Ordnance Survey Ireland

City Atlas

C000215960

CONTENTS

	PAGE
Motoring information	i
Travel information	ii
Route planner	iii
Legend to maps	iv
Cork City and District Maps	**1 - 48**
City Centre Maps	**49- 50**
Blarney / Carrigaline	51
Cobh /Ringaskiddy	52
Tourist Information	
The story of Cork	53
Buildings of note	54
Art Galleries	56
Parks and Gardens	56
Churches & Cathedrals	57
Visitor Centres	58
Towns and other places of interest...	59
Industrial Estates and Hospitals	62
Index to Street Names	63

Compiled, printed and published by Ordnance Survey Ireland, Phoenix Park, Dublin 8.
© Government of Ireland 1998

WARNING SIGNS

The following are examples of the principal signs.

| Dangerous Corner or Bend Ahead | Series of Dangerous Corners or Bends Ahead | Slippery Stretch of Road Ahead | Sharp Rise Ahead | Sharp Depression Ahead | Series of Bumps or Hollows Ahead |

Junction Ahead With Road or Roads of Equal Importance. | Steep Ascent Ahead | Steep Descent Ahead | Road Narrows Dangerously | Roundabout Ahead

Junction Ahead With Roads of Less Importance. (minor roads shown by thin arms) | Unprotected Quay, Canal or River | Road Works Ahead | Children Sign (School etc.) | Traffic Lights Ahead

Junctions Ahead With Roads of Equal Importance | With Roads of Less Importance | Advanced Warning of a Major Road Ahead | Low Bridge Ahead | Level Crossing Ahead guarded by gates. | Level Crossing Ahead Unguarded. | End of Dual Carriageway.

REGULATORY SIGNS

These signs implement road regulations and show the course to follow etc.

STOP

Give Way

YIELD RIGHT OF WAY

Traffic **must** proceed in the direction of the arrow.

Traffic **may not** proceed in the direction of the arrow.

Parking

Parking Permitted

Clearway Stopping or Parking Prohibited (except Buses and Taxis)

Parking Prohibited

TAXI RANK Parking for taxis only.

SPEED LIMITS

MOTORWAY 70 mph/112 kph.

NATIONAL LIMIT 60 mph/96 kph

OTHER LIMITS MAY APPLY IN TOWNS, BUILT-UP AREAS AND SOME ROADS AS INDICATED.

End of Speed Limit

INFORMATION SIGNS

These signs will give information regarding direction, distance, place etc. Amenities of particular interest to tourists are displayed in white on a brown background.

 4 km   2 km

Eolas do Thurasoiri TOURIST INFORMATION

↑ Loch Garman **WEXFORD** N11
← Bré **BRAY**

⚲ Motorway ahead
NO L-drivers.
Vehicles under 50 c.c.,
Slow vehicles (under 30 mph)
Invalid-carriages,
Pedal-cycles,
Pedestrians,
Animals.
Motorway ahead

↑ N11 / N7

← N81

2 Bré **BRAY**

N4 →

M50 ⚲
Entry to Motorway

← N11

Motorway Regulations no longer apply

500m
Approaching end of Motorway

BUS

Bus Átha Cliath - Dublin Bus	(01) 8734222
Bus Eireann - Irish Bus	(01) 8366111
ATHLONE	(0902) 73322
BALLINA	(096) 71800
BALLYSHANNON	(072) 51101
CAVAN	(049) 31353
CORK	*(021) 508188*
DROGHEDA	(041) 35023
DUBLIN	(01) 8366111
DUNDALK	(042) 34075
ENNIS	(065) 24177
GALWAY	(091) 562000
KILLARNEY	(064) 34777
LETTERKENNY	(074) 21309
LIMERICK	(061) 313333
LONGFORD	(043) 45208
MONAGHAN	(047) 82377
ROSSLARE HARBOUR	(053) 33114
SLIGO	(071) 60066
STRANORLAR	(074) 31089
TRALEE	(066) 23566
WATERFORD	(051) 790000

RAIL

IARNROD EIREANN - IRISH RAIL	(01) 8366222

AIR

Arrivals and departures enquiries (same day only)

DUBLIN AIRPORT	(01) 705 6705
CORK AIRPORT	
(0715- 2300 hours)	*(021) 313131*
(2300- 0700 hours)	*(021) 313288*
SHANNON AIRPORT	(061) 471444
	(061) 471666
CONNAUGHT INT. AIRPORT	(094) 67222
DONEGAL AIRPORT	(075) 48284/232
GALWAY	(091) 755569
KERRY AIRPORT	(066) 64350
SLIGO AIRPORT	(071) 68280
WATERFORD AIRPORT	(051) 75589

SEA

STENA SEALINK

DUBLIN	(01) 2047777
DUN LAOGHAIRE	(01) 2047700
ROSSLARE	(053) 33115
CORK	*(021) 272965*
LIMERICK	(061) 316259

IRISH FERRIES

DUBLIN	(01) 6610511
ROSSLARE	(053) 33158
CORK	*(021) 551995*
BRITTANY FERRIES, CORK	*(021) 277801*
SWANSEA / CORK FERRIES	*(021) 271166*

ISLE OF MAN STEAM PACKET COMPANY

DUBLIN	(01) 8741231

PAGES 1 - 48

MAIN ROADS/ STREETS

MAIN ROAD (UNDER CONSTRUCTION)

OTHER ROADS/ STREETS (UNNAMED)

NARROW / STREET PRIVATE ROAD

PEDESTRIAN STREETS

ROUTE NUMBER

BUS ROUTE

BUILT UP AREA

PUBLIC PARK etc.

PUBLIC BUILDING

RAIL/ BUS STATION

WATER

PO POST OFFICE

★ GARDA

† CHURCH

SCALE 1:10 000
(1 cm = 100 metres)

100m 50m 0 metres 100m 200m 300m 400m 500 metres

CITY CENTRE MAPS PAGES 49 - 50

MAIN ROADS/ STREETS

OTHER ROADS/ STREETS

NARROW / STREET PRIVATE ROAD

PEDESTRIAN STREETS

BUILT UP AREA

PUBLIC PARK etc.

PUBLIC BUILDING

RAIL/ BUS STATION

BUILDING OF NOTE

HOSPITAL

WATER

CINEMA

SHOPPING COMPLEX

ART GALLERY

MUSEUM

VISITOR CENTRE

LIBRARY

CHURCH OF NOTE

BUILDING OF SPECIAL INTEREST

3RD LEVEL INST. OF EDUCATION

GAELIC GROUND

RUGBY GROUND

SOCCER GROUND

THEATRE

TOURIST OFFICE

EMERGENCY HOSPITAL

INDEPENDENT HOSTEL

▲ AN ÓIGE HOSTEL

PO POST OFFICE

P PARKING

★ GARDA

FIRE STATION

MAINLINE RAIL STATION

ONE WAY TRAFFIC SYSTEM

† CHURCH

1

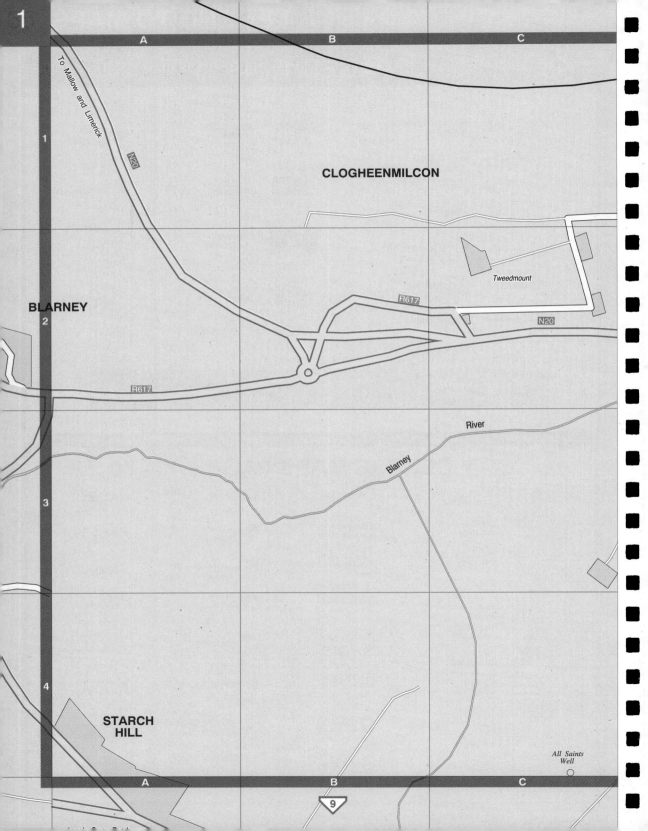

A   B   C

To Mallow and Limerick

N20

CLOGHEENMILCON

Tweedmount

R617

N20

BLARNEY

R617

River

Blarney

STARCH HILL

All Saints Well

A   B   C

D E F

1

2

3

Horgan's
Bridge

N20

Killeens Cross

The Laurels

COMMON

3

4

D E F

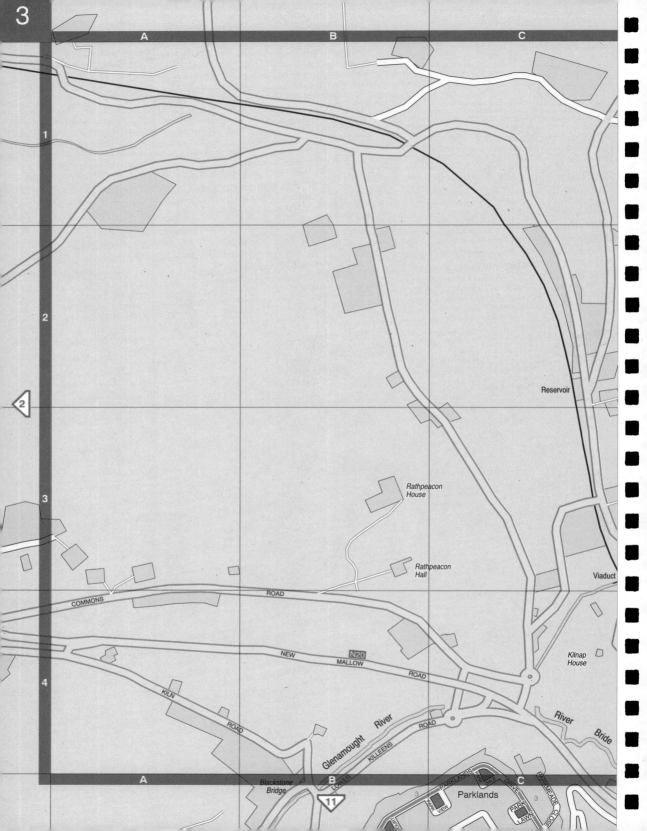

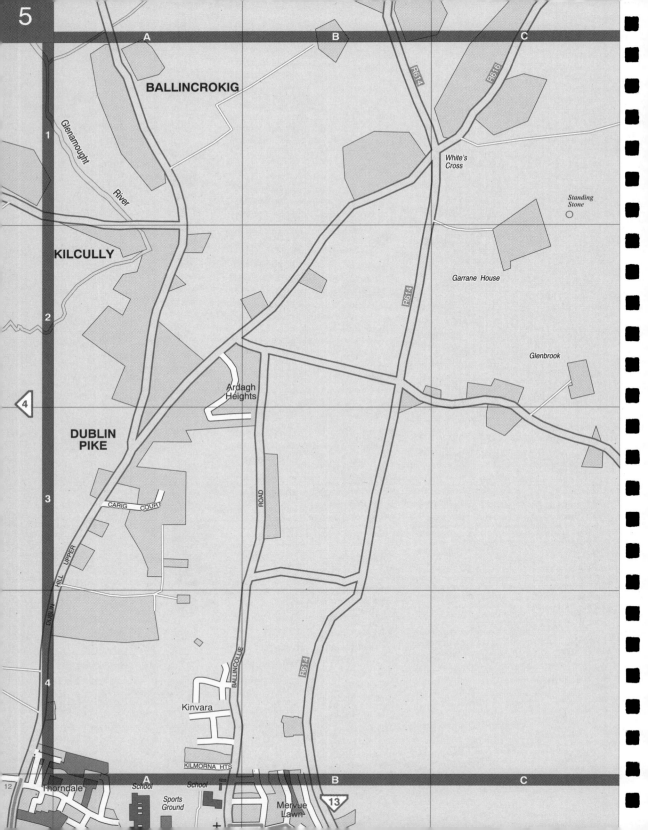

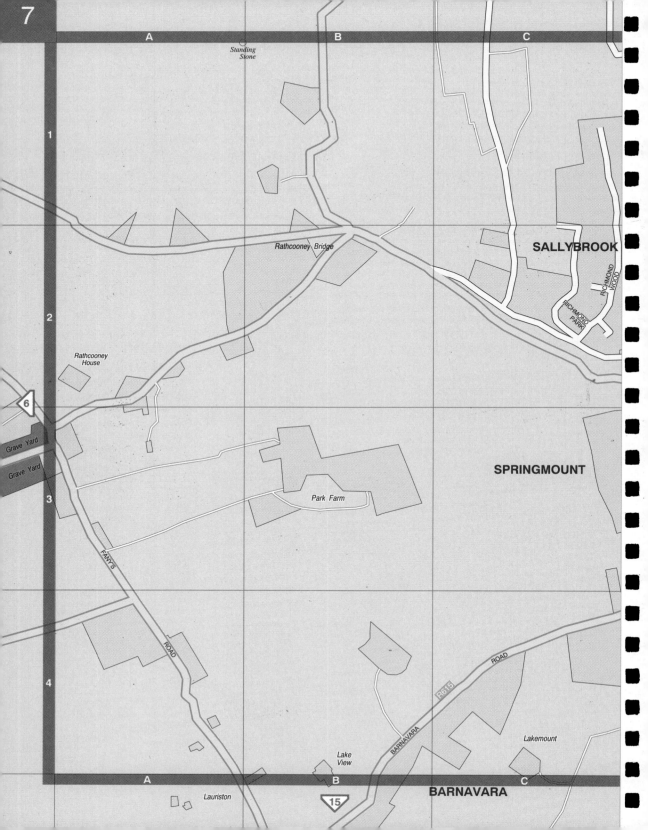

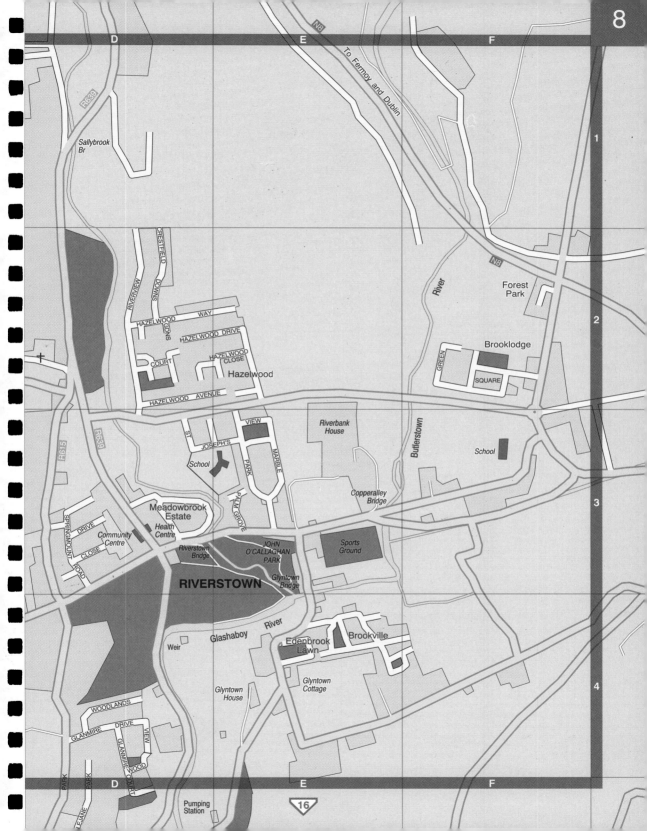

D   E   F

N8

To Fermoy and Dublin

R639

Sallybrook Br

1

N8

River

Forest Park

CRESTFIELD DOWNS

RIVERVIEW

HAZELWOOD GDNS

WAY

HAZELWOOD DRIVE

COURT

HAZELWOOD CLOSE

Hazelwood

HAZELWOOD AVENUE

GREEN

Brooklodge

SQUARE

2

Butlerstown

School

R615

R639

ST JOSEPH'S

VIEW

PARK

MARBLE

School

Riverbank House

Copperalley Bridge

3

Meadowbrook Estate

PALM GROVE

Health Centre

SPRINGMOUNT

DRIVE

Community Centre

CLOSE

ROAD

Riverstown Bridge

JOHN O'CALLAGHAN PARK

Sports Ground

RIVERSTOWN

Glyntown Bridge

Glashaboy

River

Weir

Edenbrook Lawn

Brookville

WOODLANDS

GLANMIRE

DRIVE

VIEW

GLANMIRE

WOOD

COURT

Glyntown House

Glyntown Cottage

4

PARK

LEJANE PARK

Pumping Station

D   E   F

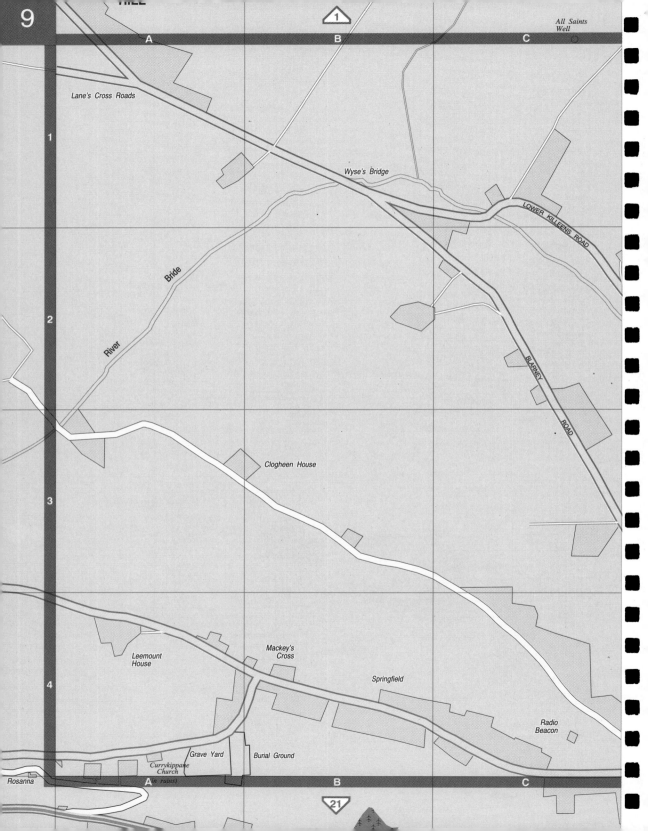

9

1

All Saints
Well

A   B   C

Lane's Cross Roads

1

Wyse's Bridge

LOWER KILLEENS ROAD

Bride

2

River

BLARNEY

ROAD

Clogheen House

3

Leemount
House

Mackey's
Cross

Springfield

4

Radio
Beacon

Grave Yard   Burial Ground

Currykippane
Church
Rosanna   (in ruins)

A   B   C

21

D E F

2

1

Killeens
House

ROAD

Templenakilleeny

KILLEENS

2

LOWER

River Bride

NASH'S BOREEN

11

3

HOLLY HILL

KILMORE

Electricty
Station

COURTOWN

2

1

HOLLYHILL

4

3

Fagothill House

BLARNEY

ROAD

Radio Beacon

Elmgrove

Halting Site

2

Ardcullen

Hollyville

D E F

Church

CLOGHEEN

22

HOLLYMOUNT
INDUSTRIAL
ESTATE

2

Sc

Sports
Ground

Cloghee

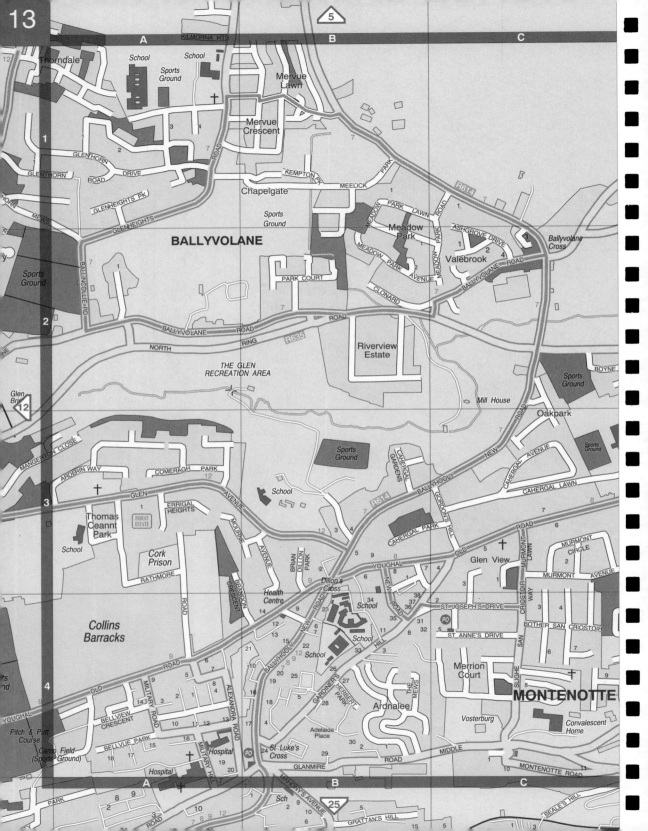

4-E1-098

4-E1-098-2023-09-26--KP

UsedGood

Cork City Street Atlas

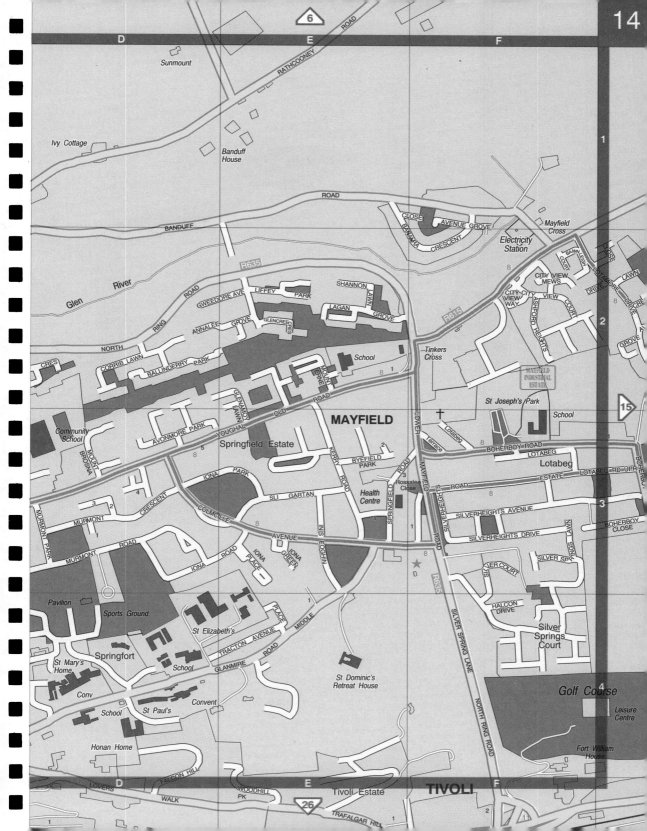

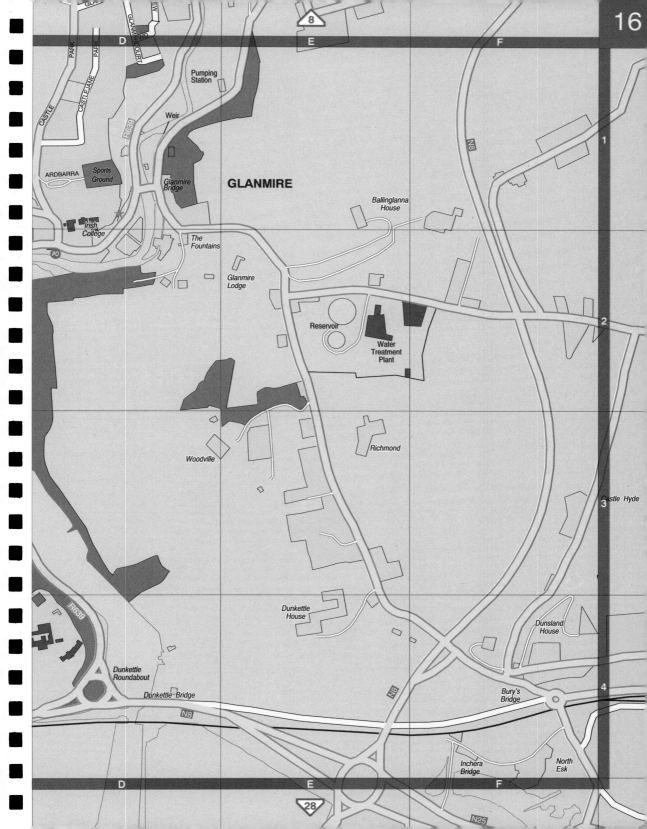

GLANMIRE

ARDBARRA

Sports Ground

Glanmire Bridge

Irish College

PO

Pumping Station

Weir

The Fountains

Glanmire Lodge

Ballinglanna House

Reservoir

Water Treatment Plant

Woodville

Richmond

Castle Hyde

Dunkettle House

Dunsland House

Dunkettle Roundabout

Dunkettle Bridge

Bury's Bridge

Inchera Bridge

North Esk

N8

N8

N8

N25

R639

R999

CASTLE PARK

CASTLEJANE PARK

GLANMIRE COURT

8

28

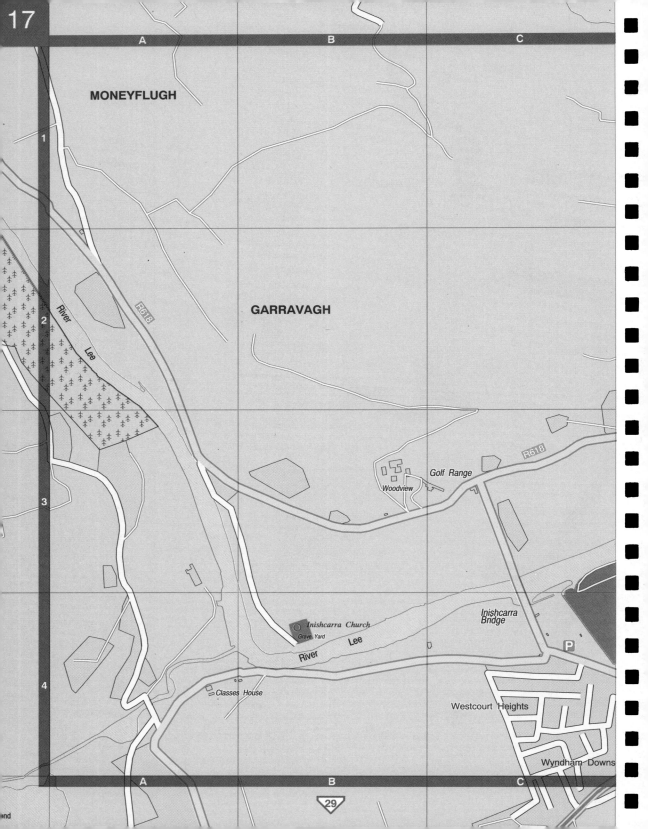

A   B   C

MONEYFLUGH

1

River

Lee

R618

2

GARRAVAGH

3

Golf Range

Woodview

R618

Inishcarra Church
Grave Yard

River   Lee

Inishcarra Bridge

P

4

Classes House

Westcourt Heights

Wyndham Downs

A   B   C

29

nd

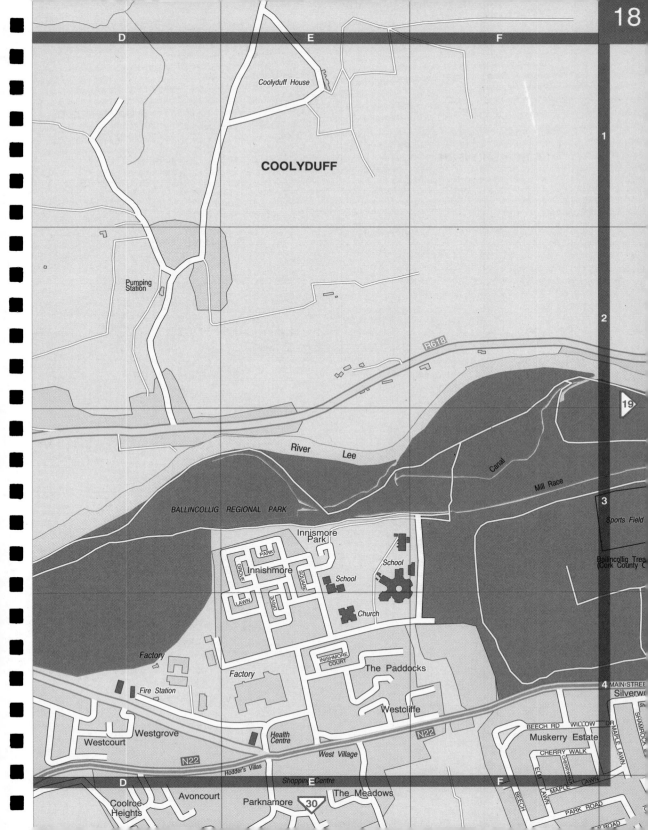

COOLYDUFF

Coolyduff House

Pumping
Station

R618

River Lee

Canal

Mill Race

BALLINCOLLIG REGIONAL PARK

Sports Field

Ballincollig Trea
(Cork County C

Innismore
Park

PARK

GROVE

Innishmore

SQUARE

DRIVE

LAWN

School

School

Church

INISHMORE
COURT

Factory

Factory

The Paddocks

Fire Station

Westcliffe

MAIN STREE
Silverw

BEECH RD

WILLOW

DR

SHAMROCK

MAPLE LAWN

Westcourt

Westgrove

Muskerry Estate

CHERRY WALK

CHERRYWALK

ELM LAWN

MAPLE LAWN

Health
Centre

West Village

N22

N22

Hodder's Villas

Coolroe
Heights

Avoncourt

Parknamore

Shopping Centre

The Meadows

30

BEECH

MAPLE

LAWN

PARK ROAD

A B C

1

GAWSWORTH

LACKENSHONEEN

TEMPLEHILL

2

R618

River Lee

18

Gunpowder Mills

Weir

Sports Ground

Sports Ground

Sports Field

Sports Ground

3

LONG RANGE

MILL RANGE

LEEVIEW

LEEVIEW

LEECOURT

Leesdale Estate

Manor Hill

Ballincollig Treatment Works
(Cork County Council)

Military Burial Ground (Disused)

LEESDALE GROVE

COURT

Glendower Court

BALLINCOLLIG

PETER O'DONOVAN CRESCENT

LEESDALE AVENUE

LEESDALE DR

School

Father Sexton Memorial Park

Rosewood

Leo Murphy Terrace

N22

Rosewood

4

MAIN STREET

Silverwood

Carrigdene

THE SQUARE

Shopping Centre

WILLOW DR

PINE WALK

STATION ROAD

Hall

Castlepark

MAPLE LAWN

SHAMROCK DRIVE

School

Church

School

Grave Yard

RRY WALK

CHERRY LAWN

MAPLE LAWN

A

B

C

PARK ROAD

CHURCH VIEW

TUDOR GROVE

STAT

31

AISLING LAWN

Beech Park

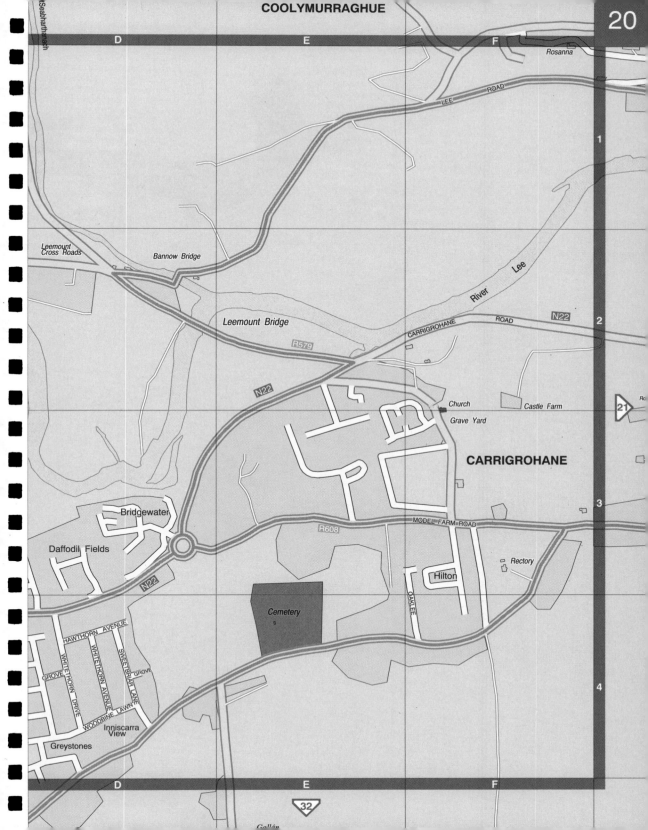

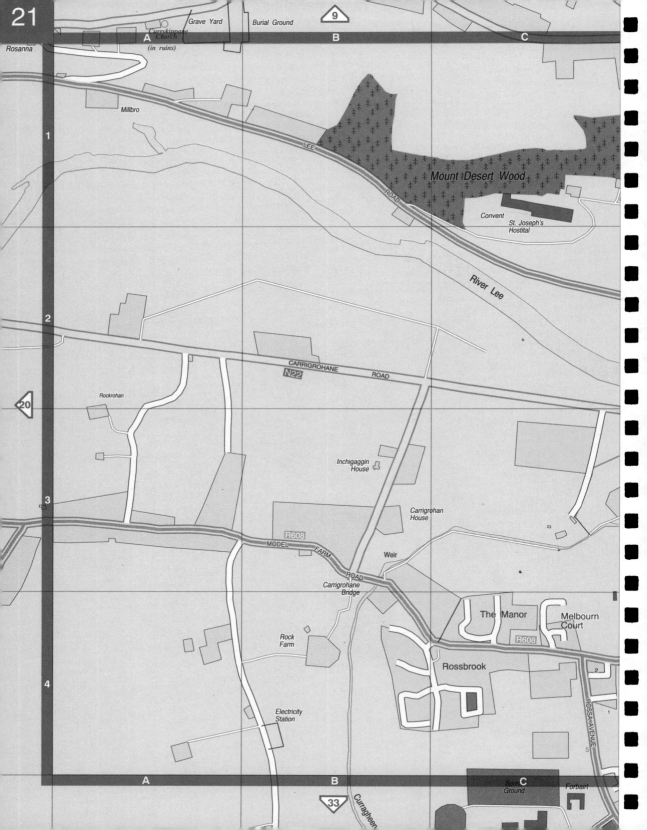

Rosanna

Currykippane Church (in ruins)

Grave Yard

Burial Ground

9

A
B
C

Millbro

LEE

ROAD

Mount Desert Wood

Convent

St. Joseph's Hostital

River Lee

1

2

20

CARRIGROHANE ROAD

N22

Rockrohan

Inchigaggin House

Carrigrohan House

3

R608

MODEL FARM ROAD

Weir

Carrigrohane Bridge

The Manor

Melbourn Court

R608

Rock Farm

Rossbrook

ROSSA AVENUE

2

1

4

Electricity Station

5

A
B
C

Spor Ground

Forbairt

33

Curragheen

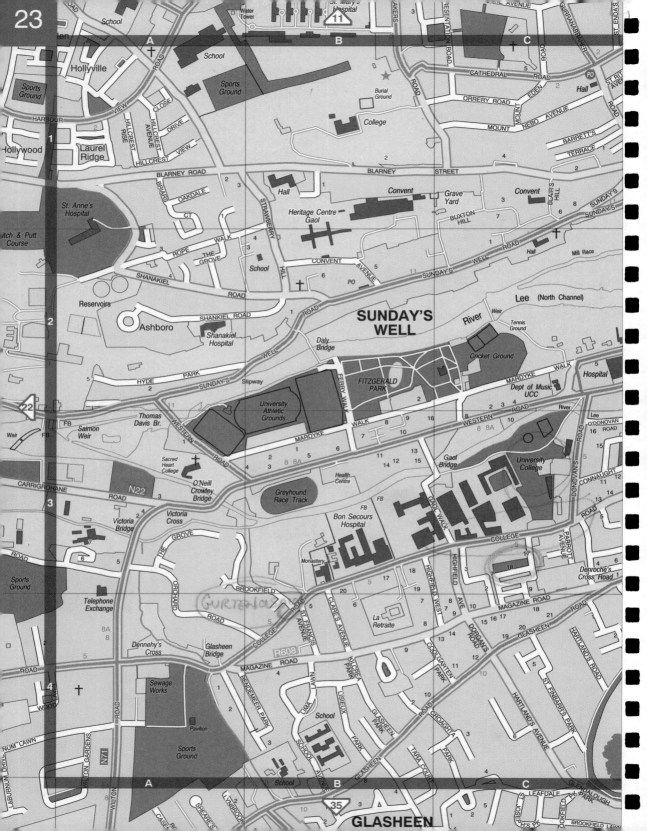

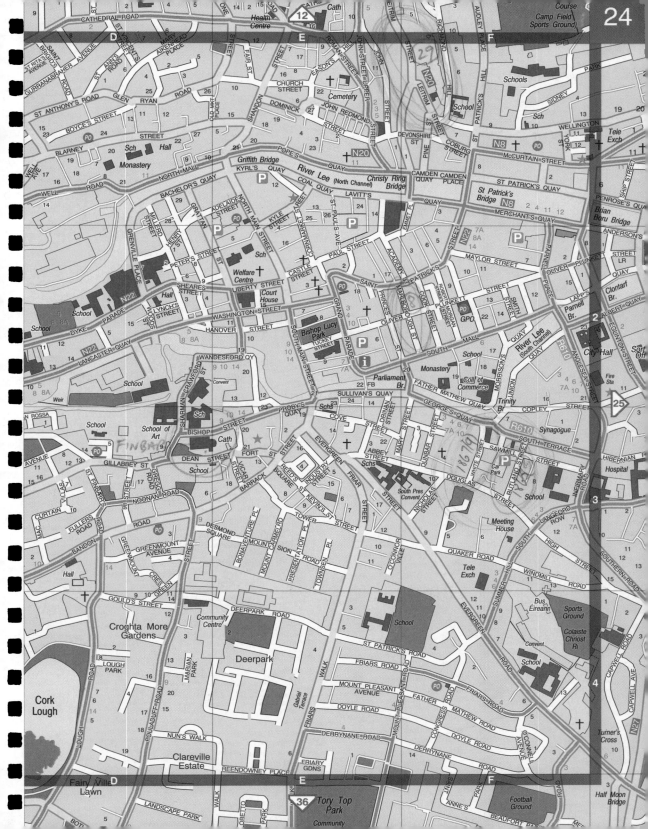

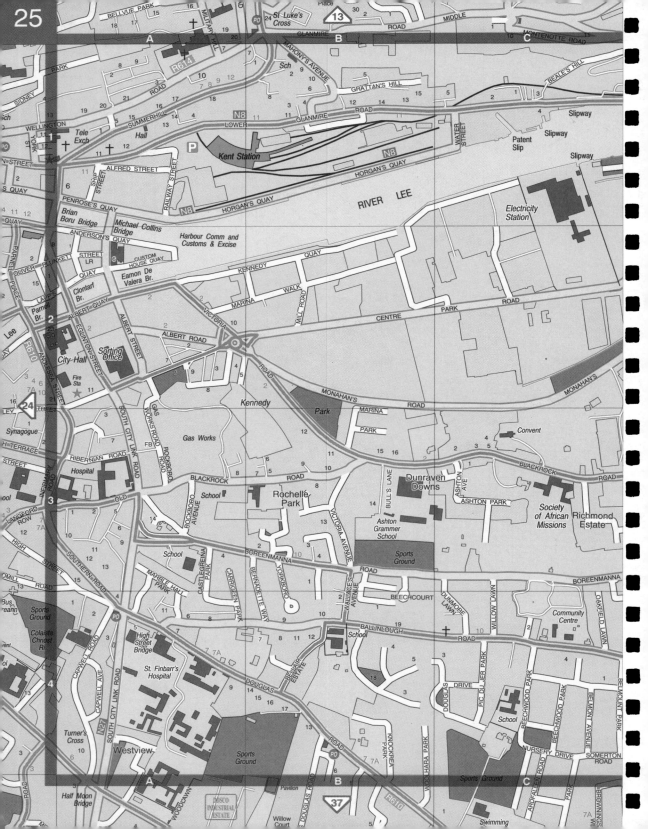

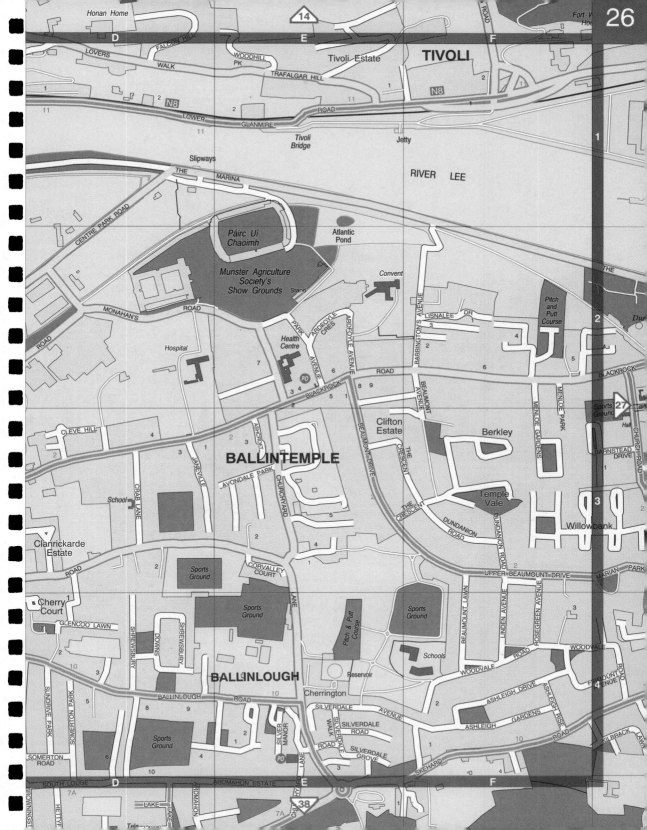

14

D E F

Honan Home
Fort W
Ho

TIVOLI

LOVERS
FALCON HILL
WOODHILL PK
WALK
TRAFALGAR HILL
Tivoli Estate

1
2
N8
2
1
1

N8
11
LOWER
GLANMIRE
ROAD
11
2
11
1
N8

Tivoli Bridge
Jetty

Slipways

THE MARINA

RIVER LEE

CENTRE PARK ROAD

Atlantic Pond

Páirc Uí Chaoimh

Convent

Munster Agriculture Society's Show Grounds
Stand

THE

Pitch and Putt Course

MONAHAN'S
ROAD
PARK
ARDFOYLE CRES
ARDFOYLE AVENUE

BARRINGTON'S AVENUE
LISNALEE DR
3

2

ROAD

Hospital

Health Centre
7

AVENUE

PO
3 4

BLACKROCK

6

ROAD
8 9
4
5
6

BLACKROCK

Sports Ground

27

BEAUMONT AVENUE
BEAUMONT PARK
MENLOE GARDENS
MENLOE PARK

Hall

CHURCH ROAD

CLEVE HILL
4

ASHCROFT

Clifton Estate

Berkley

BARNSTEAD DRIVE
1

3

2
JANEVILLE
3
1
2
3

BALLINTEMPLE

BEAUMONT DRIVE

THE CRESCENT

Temple Vale

Willowbank

School
CRAB LANE
AVONDALE PARK
CHURCHYARD
5

THE CRESCENT
DUNDANION ROAD
DUNDANION ROAD

Clanrickarde Estate
ROAD
2

Sports Ground

CORVALLEY COURT

4

1

UPPER BEAUMOUNT DRIVE
2
MARIAN PARK

Cherry Court
1
GLENCOO LAWN
2

Sports Ground

LANE

Pitch & Putt Course

Sports Ground

LINDEN AVENUE
ROSEGREEN AVENUE
3
WOODVALE

SUNDRIVE PARK
SOMERTON PARK
SHREWSBURY
SIMMONS
SHREWSBURY
10

Schools

BEAUMONT LAWN
WOODVALE ROAD

FREMOUNT AVENUE
4

BALLINLOUGH
Cherrington
Reservoir

ASHLEIGH DRIVE
ASHLEIGH RISE

SOMERTON ROAD
5
BALLINLOUGH ROAD
10
SILVERDALE AVENUE
SILVERDALE WALK
SILVERDALE ROAD
ASHLEIGH GARDENS
ASHLEIGH ROAD
KILBRACK LAWN

8
9

1
SILVER MANOR
4

Sports Ground
6

PO
SILVERDALE GROVE
3
SKEHARD
1
10
4

BROWNINGS
HETTYE
SOUTH LODGE
7A
ARDMAHON ESTATE
D E F
HY
38
LAKE
CAKE
ARDMAHON
7A
Tele

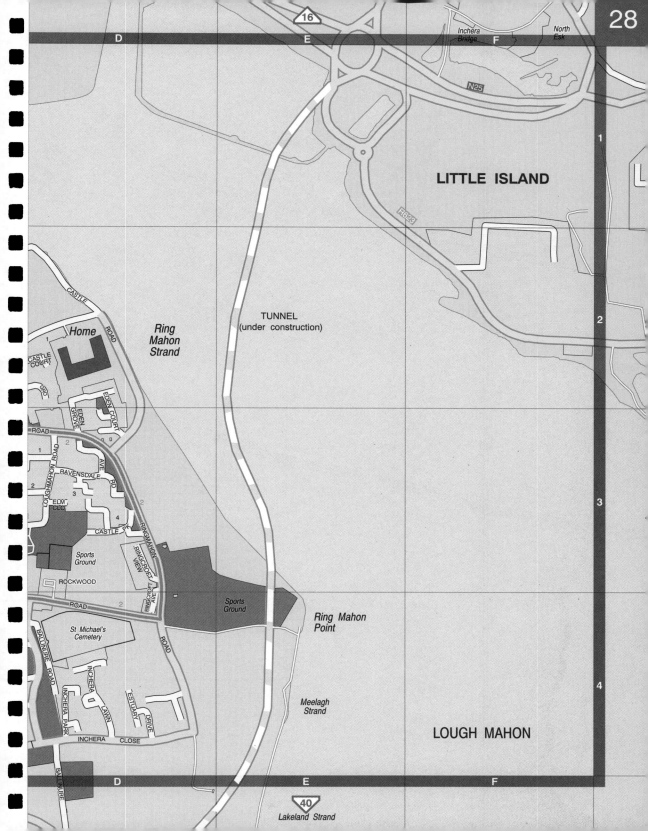

16

Inchera
Bridge

North
Esk

N25

LITTLE ISLAND

R623

1

2

CASTLE

Home

Ring
Mahon
Strand

TUNNEL
(under construction)

CASTLE
COURT

ROAD

GRO

EDEN COURT

EDEN
GROVE

ROAD

1

2

LOUGHMAHON ROAD

RAVENSDALE

AVE

RD

3

2

ELM
CLO

4

CASTLE PK

RINGMAHON

RINGCROFT
VIEW

Sports
Ground

ROCKWOOD

RINGCROFT AVE

Sports
Ground

Ring Mahon
Point

3

ROAD

2

St Michael's
Cemetery

BALLINURE ROAD

ROAD

Meelagh
Strand

LOUGH MAHON

4

INCHERA

INCHERA PARK

INCHERA LAWN

ESTUARY

DRIVE

INCHERA   CLOSE

BALLINURE

D

E

F

40

Lakeland Strand

Westcourt

N22

18 West Village

Hodder's Villas

Shopping Centre

Coolroe Heights

Avoncourt

Parknamore

The Meadows

Parknamore Rise

Cill-West Mews

Parknamore Heights

Muskerry Estate

CHERRY WALK

CHERRYWALK

ELM LAWN

MAPLE LAWN

BEECH ROAD

PARK ROAD

HOLLY ROAD

BEECH RD.

ISLAND WAY

CASTLE AVENUE

IVY CIRCLE

1

CASTLEKNO

Magl

Ballincollig Castle

2

31

3

GREENFIELD

4

D

E

F

D

E

F

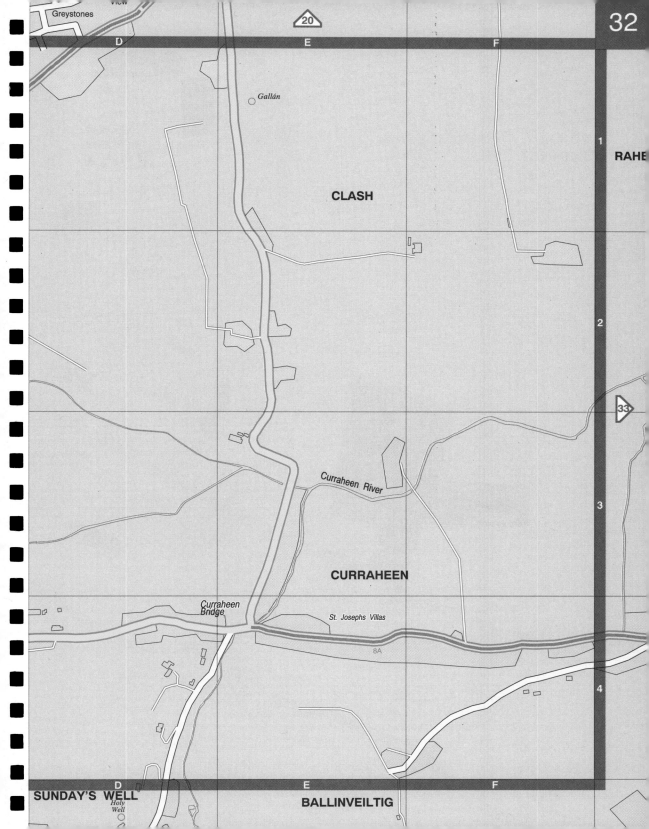

Greystones

20

D E F

Gallán

1

RAHE

CLASH

2

33

Curraheen River

3

CURRAHEEN

Curraheen Bridge

St. Josephs Villas

8A

4

SUNDAY'S WELL

Holy Well

BALLINVEILTIG

D E F

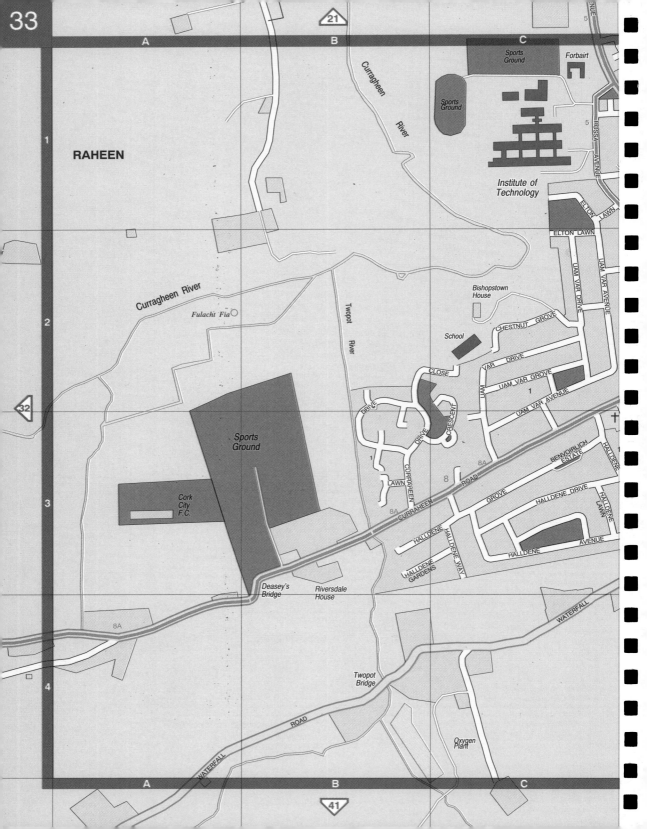

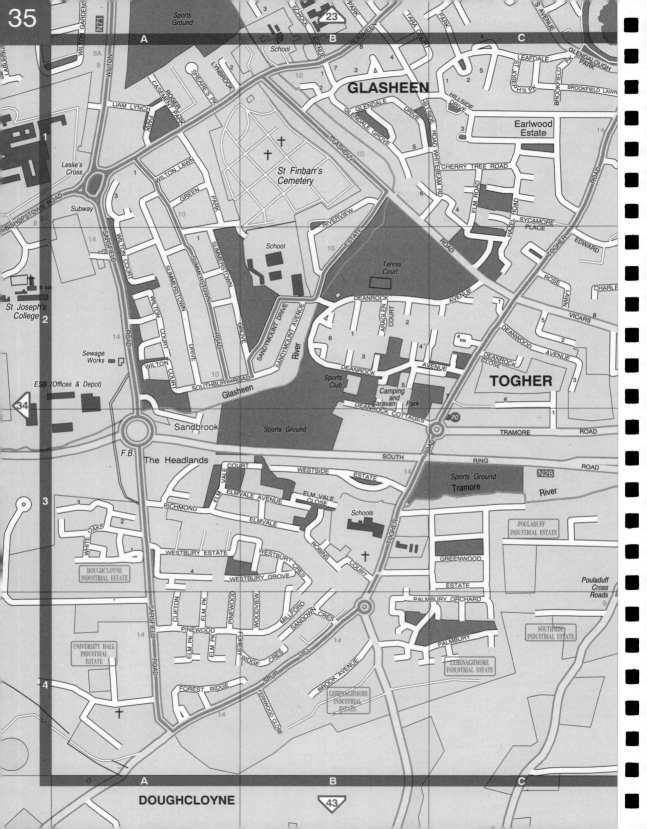

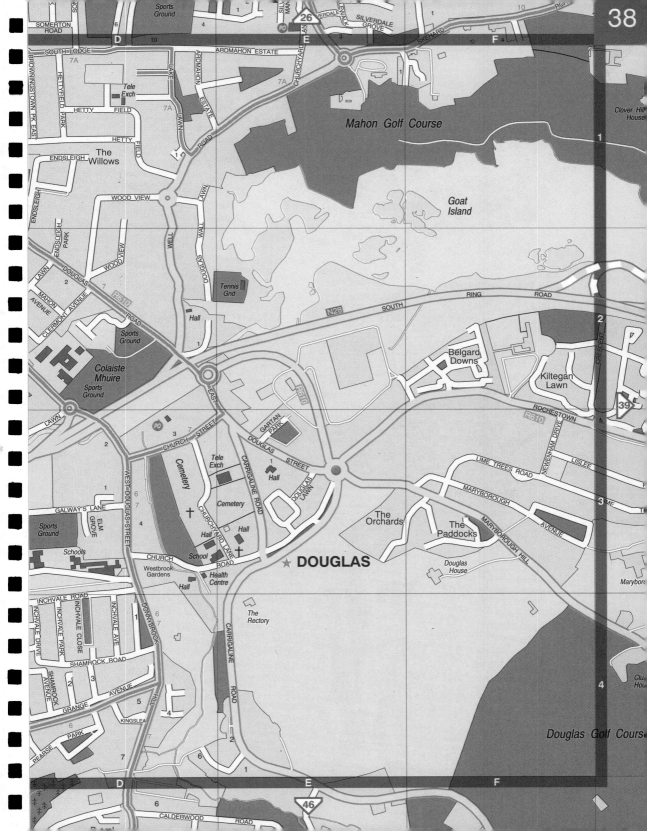

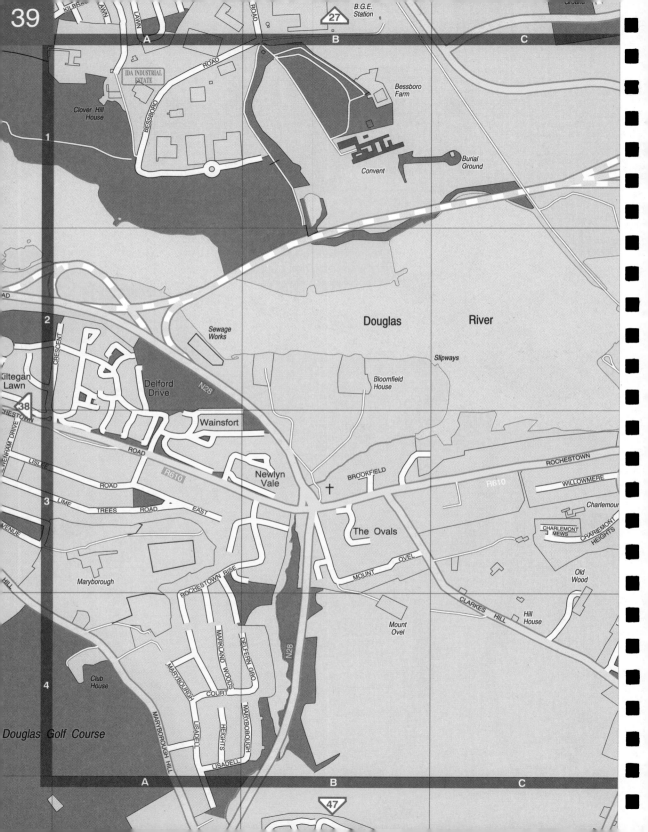

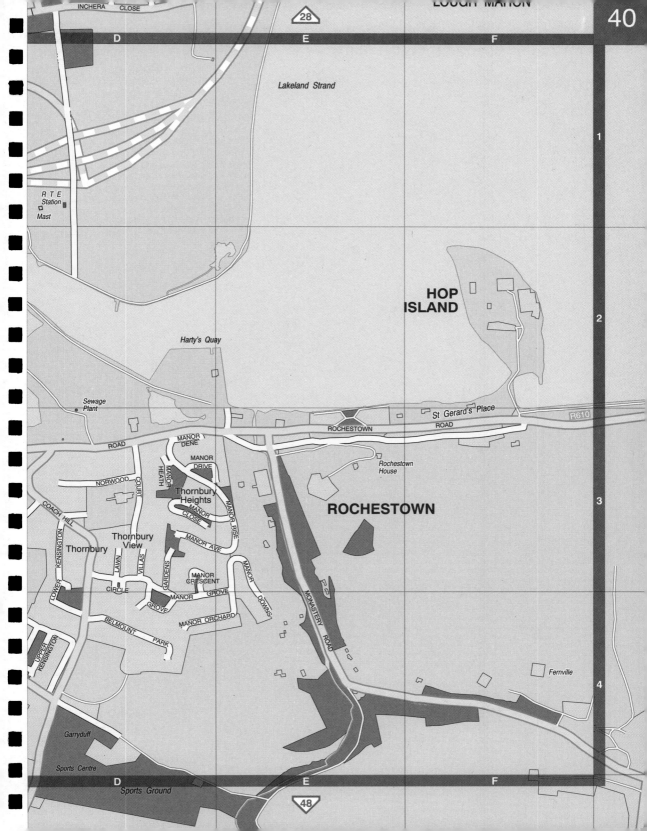

LOUGH MAHON

28

D E F

Lakeland Strand

1

R T E
Station
Mast

2

HOP
ISLAND

Harty's Quay

Sewage
Plant

St Gerard's Place

ROAD R610

ROCHESTOWN

ROAD

MANOR
DENE

MANOR
DRIVE

NORWOOD

COURT

MANOR
HEATH

Thornbury
Heights

Rochestown
House

3

MANOR
CLOSE

MANOR RISE

ROCHESTOWN

COACH HILL

Thornbury
View

MANOR AVE

Thornbury

LOWER KENSINGTON

VILLAS

LAWN

GARDENS

MANOR
CRESCENT

MANOR

DOWNS

MONASTERY ROAD

CIRCLE

MANOR GROVE

GROVE

UPPER KENSINGTON

BELMOUNT PARK

MANOR ORCHARD

Fernville

4

Garryduff

Sports Centre

D E F

Sports Ground

48

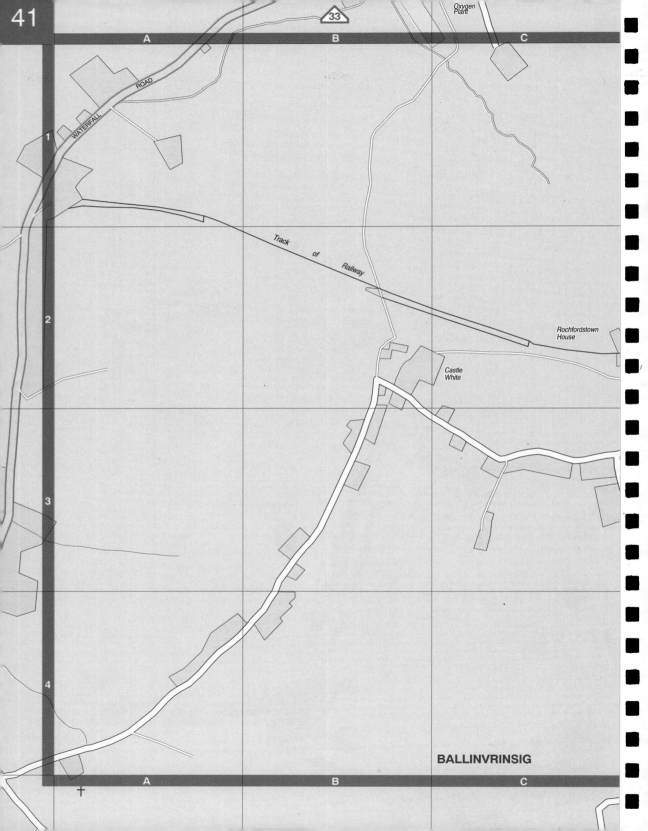

41

A   B   33   C

Oxygen
Plant

WATERFALL
ROAD

1

Track   of   Railway

2

Rochfordstown
House

Castle
White

3

4

BALLINVRINSIG

A   B   C

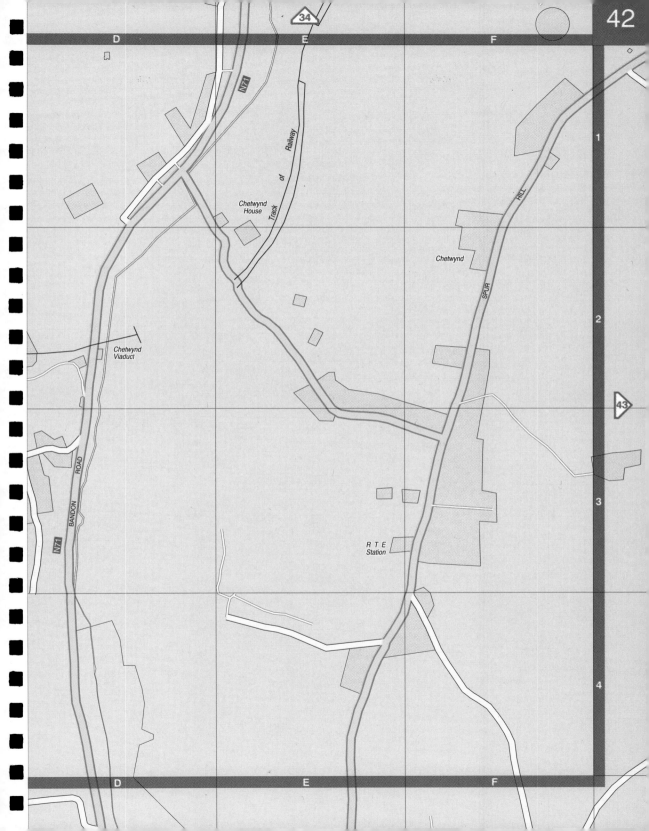

34

D
E
F

N71

1

Track   of   Railway

Chetwynd
House

HILL

Chetwynd

SPUR

Chetwynd
Viaduct

2

43

BANDON   ROAD

N71

3

R T E
Station

4

D
E
F

43

DOUGHCLOYNE

35

Philippine House

The Laurels

42

Marian House

A B C

1

2

3

4

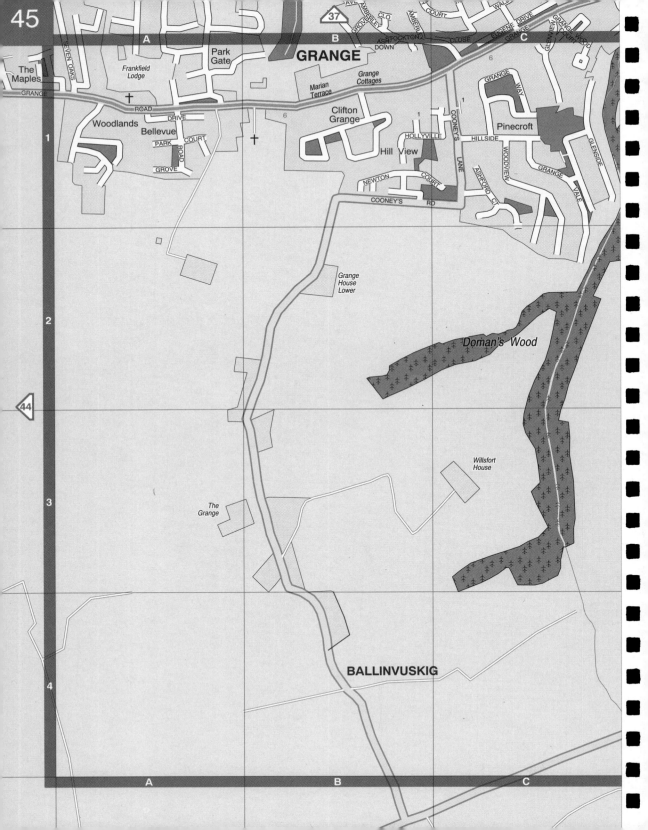

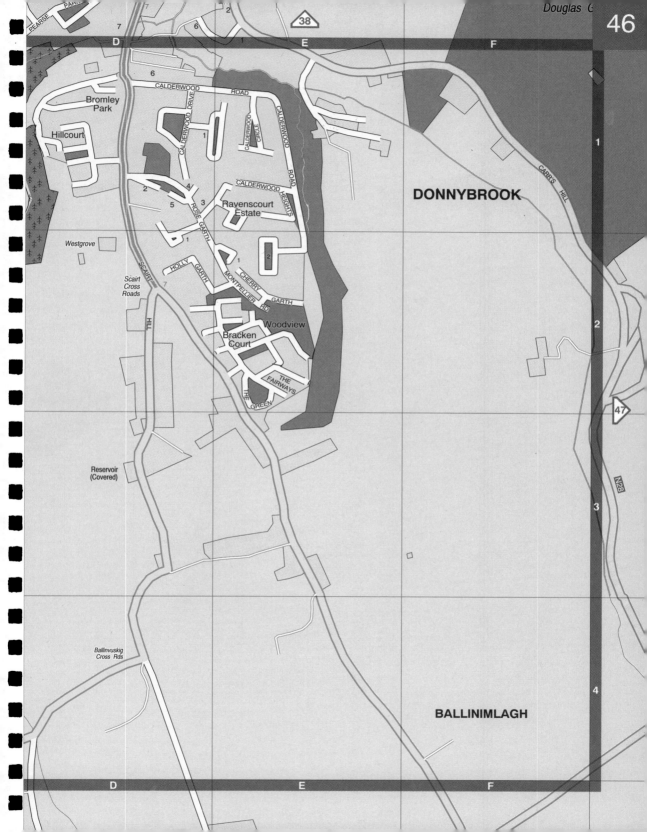

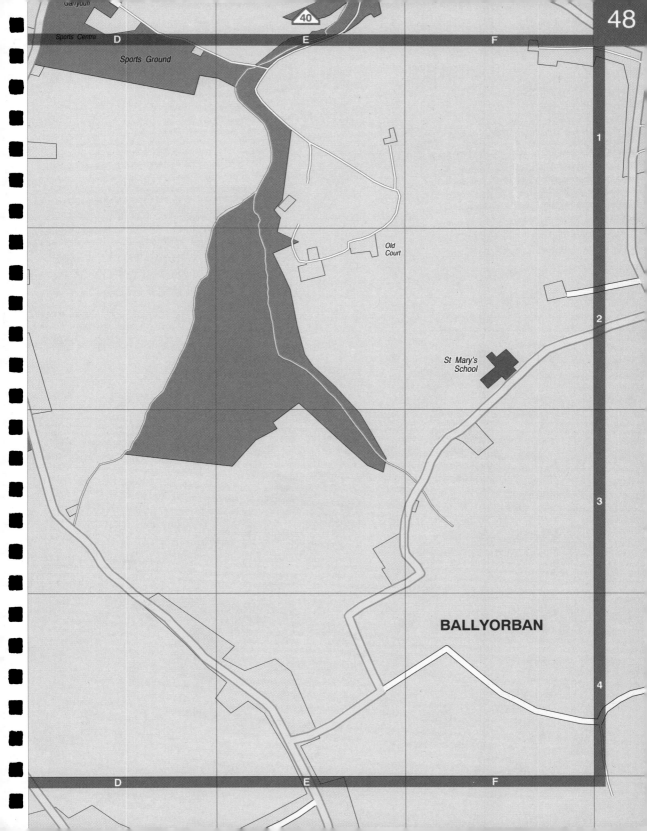

Garryduff

Sports Centre

D

Sports Ground

E

F

40

1

Old
Court

2

St Mary's
School

3

BALLYORBAN

4

D

E

F

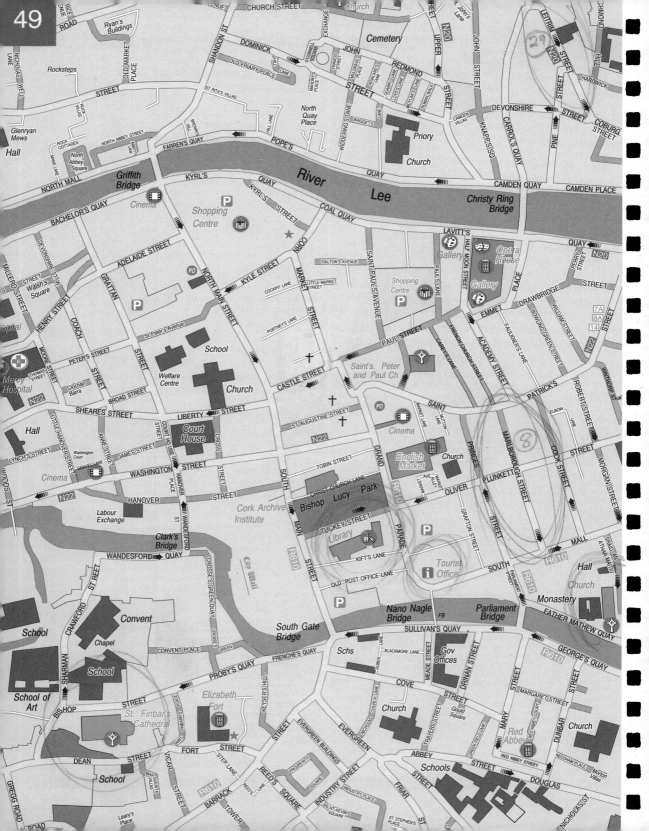

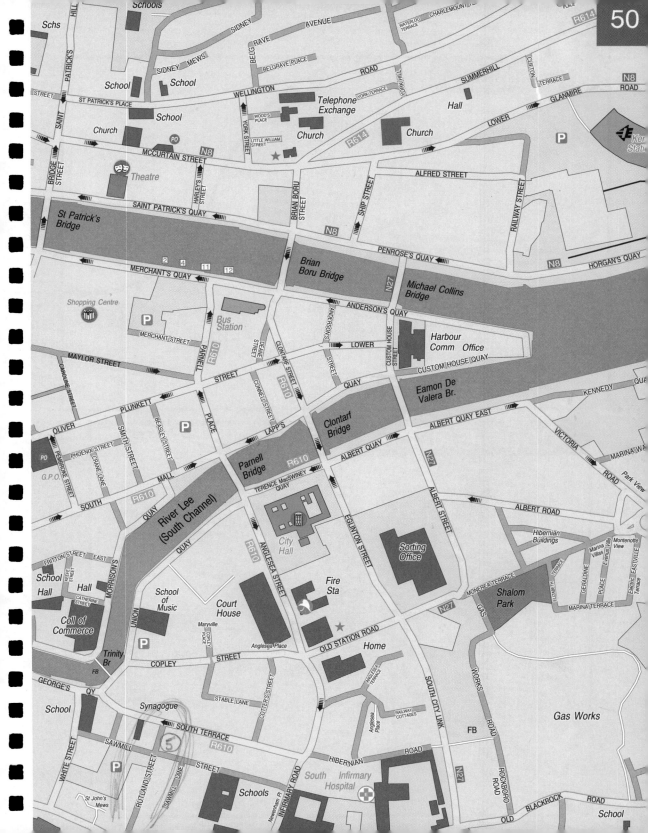

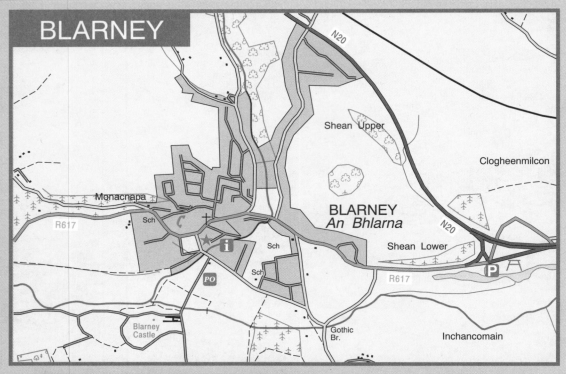

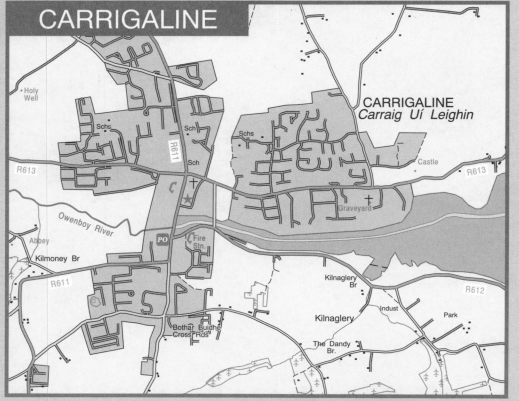

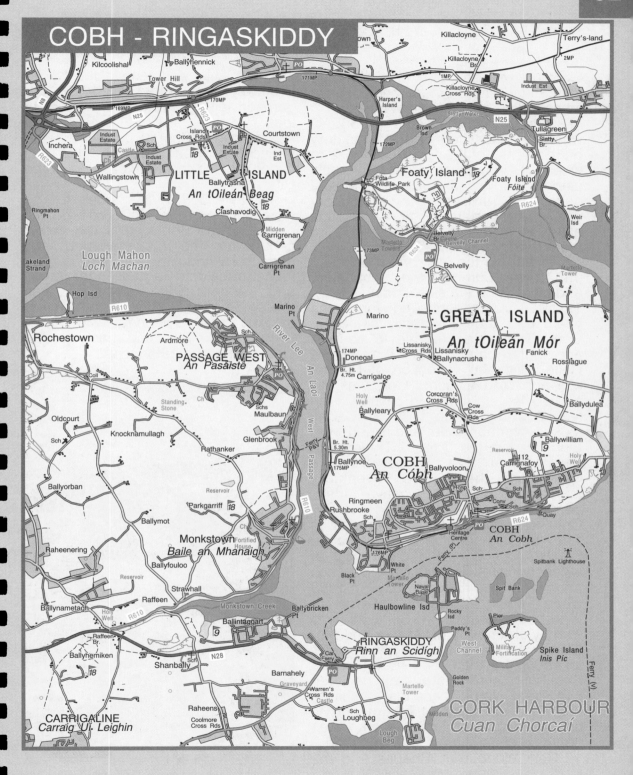

THE STORY OF CORK

Cork derives its name from Corcagh (a marshy place) where people have inhabited since pre-historic times.

Corks history begins in 595AD when St. Finbar founded a monastery on the banks of the River Lee close to where St. Finbars Cathedral now stands. A town of considerable size developed around the monastery where the cultural and religious activities of the monks flourished for more than two hundred years.

In 820AD the Norsemen attacked the town burning the monastery and plundering the surrounding area. These attacks continued for some years until they eventually settled in Cork. They later learned to co-exist and inter-marry with the native Celts. With the exception of Dermot McCarthy of Desmond, Cork was still a Danish stronghold when the Normans invaded in 1172. McCarthy took a Norman wife and sided with them against the Danes. They fell to the Norman invasion but like the Norsemen they were eventually absorbed into the native Irish population.

Cork was granted its first charter in 1185 but although it was subject to English Law it had a great deal of independence and it was the rich merchants who ruled the City. In 1493 when Peakin Warbeck, pretender to the throne arrived in Cork he was warmly greeted by the Mayor and the Elders of the City. His cause was taken up by them and they went to Kent with him where they declared him King. Warbeck and his conspirators were executed at Tyburn and in consequence of this Cork was deprived of its charter for some time.

Cork sided with Charles I in the war with his parliament but fell to Cromwell in 1649. In 1690 the garrison fell to the army of William III led by the Duke of Marlborough. Shortly after the fortification was levelled and this eventually led to the expansion of the City.

Today Cork City due to its excellent port is the commercial capital of the South. It is the export centre for the manafacturing and agricultural industries as well as the tourist trade with its passenger ferries and airport. The City is also renowned for its contribution to the Arts and Sciences with many societies some dating back to the early part of the 19th Century.

GRAND PARADE

BUILDINGS OF NOTE

QUAKER MEETING HOUSE
GRATTAN STREET
This is the building of the former Quaker Meeting House where William Penn embraced the creed before going on to the new world to found Pennsylvania.

FORMER MANSION HOUSE
HENRY STREET
This building is now the Mercy Hospital but was formerly the Mansion House for the Mayor of the City. The facade is Italianate with Venetian windows and a small Doric entrance.

THE BUTTER EXCHANGE
SHANDON
Close by, to the Church Steeple at Shandon is the site of the old Cork Butter Market. In 1770 the Cork Butter Market was opened and by 1892 the Butter Market was exporting 500,000 casks of butter all over the world. The Butter Market was finally closed in 1924.

BLACKROCK CASTLE
BLACKROCK
Built in 1830 it occupies the site of an earlier 17th century fort. It now operates as a restaurant.

UNIVERSITY COLLEGE
COLLEGE ROAD
Opened in 1849 and set in charming grounds, it was designed by Sir Thomas Deane. The Honan Chapel situated within the grounds of the University was built in 1915/1916. It is modelled on the 12th century Cormac's Chapel at Cashel. The main feature is a series of stained glass windows designed by Harry Clarke and Sarah Purser.

BLACKROCK CASTLE

CITY MARKET

CITY MARKET
The market has entrances off Grand Parade, Patrick Street and Princes Street. The origins of this market may be traced back to James I in 1610 but the present building dates from 1786.

RED ABBEY
RED ABBEY STREET
Here is the square tower of the late medieval abbey of the Canons of St. Augustine, then standing in marshland outside the eastern walls of the city. Those walls were battered from here in 1690 when the Duke of Marlborough placed a cannon on the tower. This is the oldest piece of architecture surviving in the city.

ELIZABETH FORT
off BARRACK STREET
Built in the late 16th century and converted into a prison in 1835. A part of the fort is open to the public, and commands fine views of the city from its walls.

CITY HALL
ANGLESEA STREET
This is the headquarters of Cork Corporation and City Administration. It was opened in 1936 and replaces a previous structure on the site burned down in 1920 during the War of Independence. It was associated with two honoured Lord Mayors of the City, Terence Mac Swiney and Thomas Mac Curtain.

CITY HALL

ART GALLERIES AND MUSEUMS

CRAWFORD ART GALLERY
EMMET PLACE

This gallery has an interesting frontage of red brick dressed with limestone. It was built in 1724 as the Custom House, when this street was then the King's Dock. It operated as a Custom House up to 1832 and the building was given by the Government to the Royal Cork Institution. The Institution possessed a collection of classical casts from the Vatican Galleries. The casts are still to be seen inside this Gallery.

CORK PUBLIC MUSEUM
WESTERN ROAD

Located within the grounds of Fitzgerald's Park, the museum contains a most interesting collection of exhibits which trace the history of Cork from the earliest times to the present century. The collection of very fine silver is especially important.

PARKS AND GARDENS

FITZGERALD'S PARK
WESTERN ROAD

This park is located 1.6km (1 mile) from the city centre and is bound on one side by the River Lee, and on the other by the Mardyke. The park is set on 7.25 ha (18 acres) of beautifully laid out gardens.

BISHOP LUCY PARK
GRAND PARADE

This park was opened in 1986 during the Cork 800 celebration year. Immediately inside the gates you will see a portion of the old city walls which have been excavated and restored.

BISHOP LUCY PARK

CHURCHES AND CATHEDRALS

ST. ANNE'S CHURCH
SHANDON

Central to the Shandon area is Shandon steeple, located in St. Anne's Church, which was built in 1720 and dominates the City. The pepper-pot top to the steeple is notable as is the fact that two sides of the tower are in limestone and two in sandstone. The tower contains the famous Shandon Bells, which visitors may ring. The view from the top of the steeple 37 metres (120 feet) is well worth the effort to get there.

HOLY TRINITY CHURCH
FR. MATHEW QUAY

This was commissioned in 1834 by Cork's most cherished citizen of the last century, Father Mathew, the Apostle of Temperance.

It was designed by the Pain Brothers who executed many works in Ireland for the great London architect, John Nash.

HOLY TRINITY CHURCH

ST. FINNBAR'S CATHEDRAL
BISHOP STREET

This is the Church of Ireland Cathedral in the City. On this site St. Finbar founded his monastic school about 650AD, and this school drew scholars from many parts of Europe. The Cathedral was opened in 1870, the architect being William Burgess of London, who chose the French Gothic style.

SOUTH CHAPEL
DUNBAR STREET

Built in 1776. Under the high Altar is the delicate sculpture of the 'Dead Christ' which is the work of Ireland's most distinguished sculptor of the last century, John Hogan (1800 - 1858). The marble for this piece comes from the same Carrara Quarries used by Michaelangelo.

CHURCH OF CHRIST THE KING
TURNERS CROSS

This Church at Turner's Cross is striking in it's design, and is elliptical in plan. Its length is exceeded by its width by 29 feet.

CHURCH OF CHRIST THE KING

⊙ VISITOR CENTRES

CORK CITY GAOL
SUNDAY'S WELL

The old city Gaol has been restored as a highly exciting visitor attraction which sets out to tell visitors what life was like there for prisoners in the 19th century. The building itself is of major architectural importance. An exciting audio-visual presentation is an integral part of the experience.

Also within the Gaol is the Radio Museum Experience which is situated in the former broadcasting studio 6CK. In addition to seeing the magical artifacts of early broadcasting, this exhibition deals with Marconi, the birth of radio, notable Irish and world events and broadcasting personalities.

Opening Times: (Daily)
Summer: 9.30am - 5.00pm
Winter: 10am - 4.00pm

CORK HERITAGE PARK

CORK HERITAGE PARK
BLACKROCK

Set in beautiful parkland on the outskirts of Cork city. A number of exhibitions have been developed at the Park which tell the story of the social and economic development of Cork city. The grounds at the park are open to the public and have been developed to a very high standard.

TOWNS AND PLACES OF INTEREST WITHIN REACH OF THE CITY.

BALLINCOLLIG (10KM - 6 MILES)
Ballincollig is now a major town on the western side of Cork City and is home to the Gunpowder Mills. The Mills closed in 1903 and some areas of the complex have been restored by Cork County Council.
A Powder Mills Exhibition Centre has been opened on the banks of the River Lee.

GUNPOWDER MILLS

GUNPOWDER MILLS BALLINCOLLIG
The mills were established in 1794 by Charles Henry Leslie, a leading Cork bank family. Eleven years later, when Napoleon's control of France posed a grave threat to Britain, the British Board of Ordnance bought the mills from Leslie. As well as this, the Army Barracks was built in the town to protect the supply of gunpowder. The many buildings used in the manufacture of gunpowder are still scattered along the main canal and milltracks which stretched for about a mile and a half along the bank of the River Lee.

The Gunpowder Mills Visitor Centre offers an exciting interpretation of events on the site.
Opening Times:
April to October: 10am to 6pm daily.

COBH (24KM - 15 MILES)
Cobh is situated on the southern shore of the Great Island in one of the world's natural harbours, often compared with Sydney Harbour and San Francisco Bay. The town dates from 1750 when a tiny fishing village was established on the site of the present town. As the country's premier port of call for transatlantic liners, it was for many years the point of departure for thousands of emigrants who were heading for the New World in search of a better life.

THE QUEENSTOWN STORY, COBH
Developed in portion of the Railway Station building this major visitor attraction tells the story of emigration from Ireland and Cobh to America and Australia in the period from the famine up to the 1950s. Items of special interest include sections on the loss of the liners 'Lusitania' and 'Titanic. Now Cobh's unique origins, its history and the legacy are dramatically recalled at the Queenstown Story.
Opening Times: 10am to 6pm Daily
(last admission 5pm).

GUNPOWDER MILLS

BLARNEY (10KM-6MILES)
Blarney is the home of Ireland's Crown Jewel - The Blarney Stone. Every year thousands of visitors from many countries stop off at this internationally known visitor centre to kiss the famous Blarney Stone.

BLARNEY CASTLE
The present castle with its 26 metres (85 feet) high keep was built by the McCarthy's in 1446. It replaced an earlier castle on the same site. The famous Blarney Stone is kissed by many visitors each year, and tradition says that those who kiss the stone will receive the gift of eloquence. The word 'Blarney' was introduced into the English language by Elizabeth 1, and is described as pleasant talk intended to deceive without offending.
Opening Times :
Daily throughout the year from 9am except Christmas Eve and Christmas Day.

BLARNEY HOUSE
This is one of the most elegant and gracious of the great houses of Ireland. It is a family house, now tastefully restored to its former glory.

Built in 1874, it is situated overlooking Blarney Lake and contains a collection of early furniture, family portraits, tapestries and works of art.
Opening Times:-   July   and August (Monday to Saturday) only.

BLARNEY HOUSE

FOTA WILDLIFE PARK, CARRIGTWOHILL

Fota Wildlife Park is Ireland's only Wildlife Park, and is set in gently rolling pasture land, in an area of special interest to the visitor. In this rural setting one can view rare and endangered species of wildlife, in surroundings which have been developed as close as possible to their natural environment. It was established in 1983 with the primary aim of conservation. Fota has more than 70 species of exotic wildlife in open natural surroundings with no obvious barriers.
Opening Times:
April to September 10am to 5pm
October (weekends only)
Sunday 11am to 5pm

FOTA ARBORETUM

The Fota Arboretum is possibly the finest in Ireland and contains an excellent collection of trees and shrubs from the temperate and subtropical regions of the world. Of special interest are the collections from Japan, China, South America, Australia and New Zealand. There are also collections of trees from the Himalayas and North America.
Opening Times:
As Wildlife Park

BARRYSCOURT CASTLE, CARRIGTWOHILL

Barryscourt was built in 1206. Its colourful history included for a short time the tenancy of Sir Walter Raleigh. The area surrounding the castle has been developed as a crafts centre using the existing castle out-buildings.

CARRIGALINE (13KM-8 MILES) CROSSHAVEN (6KM - 4 MILES)

Carrigaline at the Head of the Owenboy River is a busy town, and the nearest centre to the Ringaskiddy car ferry terminal. East of Carrigaline lies Crosshaven where the Owenboy River enters Cork Harbour and is one of the major international sailing centres in Ireland.

INDUSTRIAL ESTATES

ESTATES

	PAGE / GRID REF
BALLYCURREEN INDUSTRIAL ESTATE	44 E1
BLACKASH INDUSTRIAL ESTATE	36 F3
BOLANDS INDUSTRIAL ESTATE	12 D1
CORK BUSINESS AND TECHNOLOGY PARK	22 D4
DOSCO INDUSTRIAL ESTATE	37 A1
DOUGHCLOYNE INDUSTRIAL ESTATE	35 A3
FORGEHILL INDUSTRIAL ESTATE	36 D4
HOLLYMOUNT INDUSTRIAL ESTATE	22 F1
IDA INDUSTRIAL ESTATE	39 A1
KILBARRY ENTERPRISE CENTRE	4 F4
KILBARRY INDUSTRIAL ESTATE	4 F3
LEHENAGHMORE INDUSTRIAL ESTATE	35 B4
LOUGH MAHON TECHNOLOGY PARK	27 C4
MAYFIELD INDUSTRIAL ESTATE	14 F2
MILLFIELD INDUSTRIAL ESTATE	12 E1
POULADUFF INDUSTRIAL ESTATE	35 C3
SOUTHSIDE INDUSTRIAL ESTATE	35 C4
TIVOLI DOCK AND INDUSTRIAL ESTATE	27 A1
UNIVERSITY HALL INDUSTRIAL ESTATE	35 A4
YOUNGLINE INDUSTRIAL ESTATE	36 D2

HOSPITALS

	PAGE / GRID REF
BON SECOURS	23 B3
CORK UNIVERSITY HOSPITAL	34 F1
ERINVILLE LYING-IN HOSPITAL	23 C2
LINDVILLE PRIVATE MENTAL HOSPITAL	26 D2
MERCY HOSPITAL	24 D2
OUR LADY OF GOOD COUNCIL (LOTA)	16 D4
ST. ANNE'S	23 A2
ST. FINBAR'S HOSPITAL	25 A4
ST. JOSEPH'S	21 C1
ST. LUKE'S HOME	19 A4
ST. MARY'S ORTHOPAEDIC	11 B4
ST. PATRICK'S	13 A4
SHANAKIEL (SUNDAYS WELL)	23 A2
SOUTH INFIRMARY	25 A3
VICTORIA HOSPITAL	25 A3

STREET INDEX

STREET NAME	PAGE / GRID REF
A	
Abbey Street	24 E3
*Abbott's Lane	24 D1
(North Mall)	
Academy Street	24 E2
Adare Mews	38 E3.1
Adare Villas	23 C4.8
Adelaide Place	13 B4
*Adelaide Place	24 E1
(Adelaide Street)	
Adelaide Street	24 E1
Adelaide Terrace	25 A1.16
Aherlow	12 E3.7
Aisling Close	31 B1
Aisling Lawn	31 B1
Alacoque Place	23 B3.5
*Albert Place	25 A1
(on Summerhill)	
Albert Quay	25 A2
Albert Road	25 A2
Albert Street	25 A2
Aldergrove	23 B4.7
Alderwood	37 C2
Alexandra Place	13 A4.20
Alexandra Road	13 A4
*Alexandra Terrace	13 A4
(off Alexandra Road)	
Alexandra Villas	13 A4.2
Alfred Street	25 A1
Allen Square	24 D1.5
Allendale Avenue	34 D2
Allendale Drive	34 D1.3
Allevard	25 C3.3
Allinett's Lane	12 E4.8
Alma Villas	13 B4.27
Alta Place	13 B4.33
Altona	24 D3.15
Alverna	24 D2.11
Amberly	37 B4
Amberly Avenue	37 B4
Amberly Close	37 B4
Amberly Grove	37 B4
An Fhaitche	36 E2
Anderson's Quay	25 A2
Anderson's Street	25 A2.1
*Anglesea Place	25 A3.3
(off Anglesea Terrace)	
Anglesea Place	24 F2.21
Anglesea Street	24 F2
Anglesea Terrace	25 A3.3
*Anglesea Villas	24 F2
(on Anglesea Street)	
*Ann's Villas	24 E3
(Friar Street)	
Annalee Grove	14 D2
Annaville	23 B3.7
Anne Street	24 D2.4
*Annegrove	23 C3
(on College Road)	
Annmount	24 E3.10
Annville	25 B4.11
Antonia Villas	25 A3.15
*Antrim	12 F3
(off Glen Avenue)	
Araglen Court	35 B2
Arbour Court	37 B4
Ard Aluinn	13 B4.18
Árd na Greine	13 B4.19
Árd na Grena	24 F4.11
Árd na Naomh	24 D3.14
Árd na Rí Avenue	24 D4.4
Ardagh Heights	5 A2
Ardan An Riordanaigh	36 D3.1
Ardarrig Lawn	38 D4.6
Ardarrig Park	38 E4.1
Ardbarra	16 D1
Ardcairn View	26 E3.3
*Ardcairn Villas	26 E3
(on Churchyard Lane)	
*Ardcullen View	23 C4
(on Magazine Road)	
*Ardeevin	13 B4
(Gardiner's Hill)	
Ardeevin	24 D3.11
Ardeevin	25 B4.12
Arderin Way	13 A3
Arderrow Road	6 D4
Ardfallen Park	37 C1
Ardfallen Road	37 C1
Ardfallen Terrace	24 E3.17
Ardfert	12 E3.14
Ardfoyle Avenue	26 E2
Ardfoyle Crescent	26 E2
Ardfoyle Place	26 E2.6
Ardmahon Estate	38 D1
Ardmanning Avenue	36 D1
Ardmanning Lawn	36 D1.2
*Ardmichael Terrace	13 A3
(Rathmore Road)	
Ardmore Avenue	11 A4
Ardmore Avenue	23 B1.1
Ardnalee	13 B4
Ardnalee	27 A2.5
*Ardpatrick	13 B4.13
(off Frankfield View)	
Ardross Estate	24 D4.3
*Ardskeagh Villas	13 B4
(on Gardiner's Hill)	
Argideen Lawn	35 B2.5
Arthur Villas	12 E3.2
Arundel Terrace	25 B3.6
Arundel Villas	25 B3.5
Ascal San Criostoir	13 C4.3
Ascension Heights	11 B4
Ashboro	23 A2
Ashburton Hill	13 C4.2
*Ashburton Row	13 B3
(Youghal Old Road)	
Ashcroft	26 E3
Ashdale Park	37 B1
Ashdene	37 B2
Ashdown	45 B1
Ashford Court	45 C1
Ashford Estate	23 C4.4
Ashford Estate	35 C1.5
Ashford Heights	14 F2
Ashgrove Avenue	13 C2.2
Ashgrove Drive	13 C2
Ashgrove Lawn	13 C2.1
Ashgrove Park	34 D2
Ashgrove View	13 C2.4
Ashgrove Villas	13 C2.3
Ashleigh Drive	26 F4
Ashleigh Gardens	26 F4
Ashleigh Rise	26 F4
Ashton Avenue	25 C3
Ashton Cottages	25 C3.2
Ashton Park	25 C3

STREET NAME	PAGE / GRID REF
Ashton Place	13 B4.37
Ashton Place	25 C3.1
Ashton Ville	25 C3.5
Ashwood Close	12 D1.6
Assumption Road	12 F3
Auburn Villas	23 C4.17
Audley Place	12 F4
Avenue De Rennes	27 C3
*Avoca	12 F3
(off Glen Avenue)	
Avoncourt	30 D1
Avondale	23 C2.3
Avondale Park	26 E3
Avonlea Court	26 A3
Avonlea Gardens	27 A4.3
Avonlea Row	27 A3.2
Avonmore Park	14 D3
Aylsbury	29 C1
Aylsbury Avenue	29 C1
Aylsbury Court	29 C1
Aylsbury Crescent	29 C1
Aylsbury Downs	29 C1
Aylsbury Lawn	29 C1

B

STREET NAME	PAGE / GRID REF
Bachelor's Quay	24 D1
Baker's Road	11 B4
Ballinaspig Lawn	34 E1
Ballincollie Park	13 A2.1
Ballincollie Road	5 A4
Ballincollie Road	13 A2
Ballincollig	19 A4
Ballincrokig	5 A1
Ballincurrig Park	37 C1
Ballinderry Park	14 D2
Ballinimlagh	46 F4
Ballinlough	26 E4
Ballinlough Road	25 B4
Ballinsheen Court	27 B3
Ballintemple	26 E3
Ballinure	27 C2
Ballinure Avenue	27 C4
Ballinure Cottages	27 C4
Ballinure Crescent	27 C3.1
Ballinure Lawn	27 C4.1
Ballinure Place	27 B4

STREET NAME	PAGE / GRID REF
Ballinure Road	27 C3
Ballinure Road	28 D4
Ballinvrinsig	41 C4
Ballinvuskig	45 B4
Ballybrack Heights	38 D4.4
Ballycurreen Road	44 E1
Ballyhooly New Road	13 B4
Ballymacthomas Street	24 D1.4
Ballyorban	48 F4
Ballyphehane	36 F2
Ballyvolane	13 A2
Ballyvolane Road	13 A2
Balmoral Terrace	13 B4.14
Baltimore Lawn	37 B1.5
Bandon Road	24 D3
Banduff Road	14 D1
Bantry Park Road	11 C3
Barnavara	15 C1
Barnavara Avenue	14 F1
Barnavara Close	14 E1
Barnavara Crescent	14 F2
Barnavara Grove	14 F1
Barnavara Road	7 B4
Barnstead Avenue	27 A3.1
Barnstead Drive	27 A3
Barrack Street	24 E3
Barrett's Buildings	23 C1.1
Barrett's Lane	34 E3
*Barrett's Lane	13 A4
(Military Road)	
Barrett's Terrace	23 C1
Barrington's Avenue	26 F2
Barry's Lane	25 B1.3
*Barry's Place	12 E3
(Seminary Road)	
Bawnleigh Court	14 F2
Beachwood Place	25 B4.17
Bealach San Criostoir	13 C4.4
Beale's Hill	25 C1
Beasly Street	24 F2.12
Beaufort Park	36 F1
Beaumont Avenue	26 F2
Beaumont Cottages	26 E3.4
Beaumont Drive	26 E3
Beaumont Lane	26 E2.1
Beaumont Place	26 E2.9

STREET NAME	PAGE / GRID REF
Beaumount Court	26 F4.3
Beaumount Lawn	26 F4
*Beech Ville	24 D4
(on Lough Road)	
Beech Park	31 B1
Beech Road	18 F4
Beech Road	30 F1
Beechcourt	25 B3
Beechmount Place	25 A1.7
Beechwood Close	27 C2.3
Beechwood Court	27 C2.4
Beechwood Drive	25 B4.1
Beechwood Grove	12 D1
Beechwood Grove	12 D1.4
Beechwood Park	25 C4
Beechwood Road	27 C2
Belgard Downs	38 F2
Belgrave Avenue	24 F1.4
Belgrave Place	24 F1.13
Bellair Estate	25 B4
Bellavista	23 C4.10
*Bellevue	23 A2
(off Western Road)	
Bellevue Court	45 A1
Bellevue Drive	45 A1
Bellevue Grove	45 A1
Bellevue Park	45 A1
Bellevue Road	45 A1
Bellevue Terrace	13 A4.9
Bellview Crescent	13 A4
Bellvue Park	13 A4
Bellvue Terrace	13 A4.15
Bellvue Villas	26 D1.2
Belmont Avenue	25 C4
Belmont Park	25 C4
Belmont Place	25 B4.14
Belmont Terrace	13 B4.21
Belmount Park	40 D4
Belvedere Lawn	37 C2
Bendemeer Park	23 B4
Benvoirlich Estate	33 C3
Berkeley Court	37 B2.1
Berkley	26 F3
Berlingford Drive	26 A3
Bernadette Place	23 B3.6
Bernadette Way	25 B3

STREET NAME	PAGE / GRID REF	STREET NAME	PAGE / GRID REF	STREET NAME	PAGE / GRID REF
Berwick Lane	12 E3[10]	Bóthar Mac Piarais	36 D1	Brother Rice Avenue	24 D1[3]
Bessboro Road	27 B4	Bóthar Ó Conghaile	36 D2	Brown's Hill	24 E1[20]
Bessboro Road	39 A1	Bóthar San Criostoir	13 C4	Browningstown Park	37 C1[3]
*Bethseda Row	25 A3	Bóthar na mBlath	36 F1	Browningstown Park E.	38 D1
(on Old Blackrock Road)		Bóthar na mBuaircini	36 E1	Browningstown Park W.	37 C1
Beverly Drive	34 D2	Bóthar Ó Cleirigh	36 E1	Bryan Terrace	25 B4[19]
Birch Place	35 B1[6]	Bowling Green Street	24 F2[6]	*Buckingham Place	24 F2
Birchwood Close	12 D1[2]	Boyce's Street	24 D1	(on Georges Quay)	
Bishop Street	24 D3	Boyne Crescent	13 C2	Buckley's Terrace	24 D1[13]
Bishopscourt Avenue	34 E2[2]	Bracken Court	46 E2	Bull's Lane	25 E3
Bishopscourt Drive	34 F2	Braemar	25 A3[8]	*Bunker's Hill	12 C4
Bishopscourt Green	34 F2	Bramble Cottages	12 E2[5]	(on St Mary's Road)	
Bishopscourt Hill	34 E1[1]	Brampton Court	34 E3	Burke's Avenue	12 E4[4]
Bishopscourt Lawn	34 E2	Brandon Crescent	13 A3	Burke's Hill	15 B4
Bishopscourt Park	34 F2[1]	Brendan Ville	23 C4[12]	Burton Place	13 B4[36]
Bishopscourt Place	34 F2[2]	Brentwood Court	35 A3[2]	Buxton Hill	23 C1
Bishopscourt Road	34 F1	Brian Boru Street	25 A1[6]	*Buxton Terrace	23 B2
Bishopscourt Way	34 F2[3]	Brian Dillon Crescent	13 C4[5]	(on Sunday's Well Road)	
Bishopstown	34 D1	Brian Dillon Park	13 B3	Byefield Court	14 E3[2]
Bishopstown Avenue	22 F4	Briars Court	23 A1	Byefield Park	14 E3
Bishopstown Avenue W.	34 F1	Bride Villas	12 D1[9]		
Bishopstown Park	22 F4[2]	Bridevalley Park	11 C2	**C**	
Bishopstown Road	34 E2	Bridevalley View	11 C2		
Blackash Road	36 F2	Bridge Street	24 F1[8]	Cahergal Avenue	13 C3
Blackmore Lane	24 E2[24]	*Bridgeview	23 A2	Cahergal Gardens	13 B3
Blackpool	12 F3	(on Sunday's Well Road)		Cahergal Lawn	13 C3
Blackpool Bridge	12 E3[20]	Bridge View Heights	4 E4	Cahergal Park	13 B3
Blackrock	27 C2	Bridgeview Terrace	23 A3[5]	Cahergal Terrace	13 B3[9]
Blackrock Road	25 C3	Bridgewater	20 D3	Cahergal Villas	13 B3[4]
Blackrock Road	27 A2	Brighton Villas	23 B3[12]	Cahill Ville	13 A4[7]
Blackwater Grove	35 B2[3]	Broad Lane	12 E3[11]	Cairn Court	22 E4
Blair's Hill	23 C1	Broad Street	24 D2[9]	Calderwood Circle	46 E1
Blair's Hill Square	23 C1[6]	Broadale	47 B1	Calderwood Court	46 D1[1]
Blarney Road	10 D3	Brocklesby Street	12 E3[3]	Calderwood Drive	46 D1
Blarney Road	22 E1	Broguemakers Hill	24 E1[15]	Calderwood Heights	46 E1
Blarney Road	23 A1	Bromley Park	46 D1	Calderwood Road	46 D1
Blarney Street	24 D1	Brook Avenue	35 B4	*Calville	24 D3
Blarney View	13 B4[8]	Brookfield	23 A3	(on Bandon Road)	
Bleasby's Street	12 E4[7]	Brookfield	39 B3	*Cambridge Place	13 B4
Bloomfield Terrace	23 B3[13]	Brookfield Lawn	35 C1	(on Gardiner's Hill)	
Boherboy Close	15 A3	Brookfield Mews	23 B4[6]	Camden Place	24 F1
Boherboy Road	14 F3	Brookfield Park	35 C1	Camden Quay	24 F1
Bonaventure Place	24 E3	Brookfield Villas	23 B3[20]	*Camden Villas	24 E1
Boreenmanna Road	25 A3	Brooklodge Green	8 F2	(off John Redmond Street)	
Boston Park	36 D1	Brooklodge Square	8 F2	Capwell Avenue	25 A4
Bóthar Ceannt	36 E1	Brookville	8 E4	Capwell Road	25 A4
				Carbery Grove	11 B4

STREET NAME	PAGE / GRID REF	STREET NAME	PAGE / GRID REF	STREET NAME	PAGE / GRID REF
Cardinal Court	34 F2	Castleview Terrace Lr.	25 C1.4	Church Road	38 D3
Cardinal Way	34 F2	Castlewhite Apartments	23 B3.14	Church Street	24 E1
Carey's Lane	24 E2.1	Cathedral Avenue	24 E1.17	Church Street	38 D3
Carig Court	5 A3	*Cathedral Place	24 D3	Church View	31 A1
*Carlisle Terrace	23 A2	(on Bishop Street)		Churchfield Avenue	11 C4
(off Sunday's Well Road)		Cathedral Road	12 D4	Churchfield Gardens	11 C3.1
Carmelite Place	23 B3.4	Cathedral Street	12 E4.16	Churchfield Green	11 B4
Carnog Mac Piarais	36 D1.1	Cathedral Walk	12 E4	Churchfield Hill	11 C4
Carolina Terrace	13 B4.30	*Catherine Street	24 F2	Churchfield Place East	11 C4
Caroline Street	24 F2.11	(off Morrison Quay)		Churchfield Place West	11 C4.1
Carr's Hill	46 F1	Cattle Market Avenue	24 E1.10	Churchfield Road	11 C3
*Carrig Side	23 C3	Ceanncora Lawn	26 D3.2	Churchfield Square	11 C3
(on College Road)		Cedar Avenue	34 E2	Churchfield Terrace West	11 C4.2
Carrig View Terrace	25 A3.5	*Cedar Grove	23 C4	Churchfield Terrace East	11 C4
Carrigaline Road	38 E3	(on Glasheen Road)		Churchfield Way Lower	11 C4
Carrigaline Road	38 E4	Cedar Grove	34 E2	Churchfield Way Upper	11 B3
Carriganarra	31 B1	Centenary Crescent	24 D4.9	Churchyard Lane	26 E3
Carrigdene	19 B4	Centenary Row	13 A4.6	Churchyard Lane	38 E1
Carrigdhun	23 C2.5	Central Avenue	34 E1	Churchyard Lane	38 D3
Carrigdubh Estate	26 F2.5	Centre Park Road	25 B2	Citi-West Mews	30 E1
Carrigeen Park	25 A3	Chapelgate	13 A1	City View	13 B4.5
Carrigfern	23 B3.17	*Chapel Hill	12 E4.16	City View Court	14 F2
*Carriglee	23 C3	(off Cathedral Street)		City View Mews	14 F2
(off Western Road)		Chapel Street	24 E1.9	City View Way	14 F2
Carrigmore Park	26 E4.2	Charlemont Heights	39 C3	Clahane Cottages	25 B1.14
Carrigrohane	20 F3	Charlemont Mews	39 C3	Clanrickarde Estate	26 D3
Carrigrohane Road	22 E3	Charlemont Terrace	25 A1.3	*Clarence Court	25 B1.2
*Carroll's Place	24 E1	Charles Daly Road	35 C2	(off Clarence Terrace)	
(off John's St Upper)		Charleville Cottages	13 A4.5	*Clarence Lodge	25 B1.2
*Carroll's Lane	24 E1	Cherrington	26 E4	(off Clarence Terrace)	
(off John Street)		Cherry Court	26 D4	*Clarence Place	25 A1
Carrolls Quay	24 F1.1	Cherry Drive	25 B4.6	(off Summerhill)	
Castle Avenue	26 F1.2	Cherry Gardens	46 D2.1	Clarence Terrace	25 B1.2
Castle Avenue	31 A1	Cherry Garth	46 E2	Clareville Estate	24 D4
Castle Avenue	27 C2	Cherry Grove	22 E4	Clark's Bridge	24 E2.19
Castle Court	28 D2	Cherry Grove	46 D1.5	Clarke's Hill	39 C4
Castle Park	16 D1	Cherry Tree Road	35 C1	Clash	32 E1
Castle Park	28 D3	Cherry Walk	18 F4	Clashduv Place	35 B1.7
Castle Road	27 B2	Chesterton Close	25 B4.3	Clashduv Road	35 B1
Castle Street	24 E2	Chestnut Grove	33 C2	Clashduv Terrace	35 B1.8
Castlegreina Park	25 A3	Chiplee Villas	26 D3.4	Clashduv Villas	35 B1.1
Castlejane Park	16 D1	Christ Church Lane	24 E2.8	*Clermont Cottages	37 C2
Castleknock	31 A1	Church Hill	15 C1	(on Sth Douglas Rd)	
Castlepark	19 B4	Church Avenue	12 E4.10	*Clermont Terrace	37 C2
Castleview	31 B1	Church Avenue	27 A2	(on Sth Douglas Rd)	
Castleview Terrace	25 C1.5	Church Road	27 A3	Clermont	38 D2.2

STREET NAME	PAGE / GRID REF	STREET NAME	PAGE / GRID REF	STREET NAME	PAGE / GRID REF
Clermont Avenue	38 D2	Convent Avenue	23 B2	Croaghta Park	23 C4
Cleve Hill	26 D3	Convent Avenue	27 B2.3	Croghtamore Gardens	24 D4
Clifton	35 A4	Convent Lane	22 F4.1	Croghtamore Square	23 C4.1
Clifton Avenue	13 C4.7	Convent Mews	27 B3.1	Crones Lane	24 E3.12
Clifton Estate	26 E3	Convent Place	12 E4.2	Cross Douglas Road	37 B1
Clifton Grange	45 B1	Convent Place	24 E2.13	*Cross Lane	12 F3
Clifton Road	13 C4.6	Convent Road	26 B2	(off Dublin Street)	
Clifton Terrace	25 A1.4	Convent View	23 A1.3	*Cross Lane	24 E3
Clifton View	26 E2.8	*Convent View Tce	23 B1	(off Barrack Street)	
Clochán Barra	24 D2.6	(off Strawberry Hill)		Cross Street	24 E2.15
Clogheen	22 F1	*Conway's Lane	24 D1	Cross's Green	24 E2.12
Clogheenmilcon	1 B1	(off Blarney Street)		Cross's Green Quay	24 E2.20
Clonard	25 C3.4	Cook Street	24 F2	Curragh Road	36 F1
Clonard	13 B2	Coolgarten Park	23 B4	Curraheen	32 E3
Clontarf Estate	27 A4	Coolmaine Crescent	10 F4.1	Curraheen Close	33 B2
Clontarf Street	24 F2.8	Coolowen Villas	23 B4.4	Curraheen Crescent	33 C2
Clontymon Lawn	25 B3.2	Coolroe Heights	30 D1	Curraheen Drive	33 B2
Close's Green	12 D2.3	Coolyduff	18 E1	Curraheen Lawn	33 B3
Close's Park	12 D2.4	Cooney's Road	45 B1	Curraheen Road	33 B3
Close's Road	12 D3	Cooney's Lane	45 C1	Curraheen Road	34 D2
Clover Hill Estate	27 A4	Copley Place	24 F2.16	Curry's Rock	24 E1.11
Clover Lawn	27 A4	Copley's Street	24 F2	Cushing Place	12 E2
Cnoc Mhuire	12 E4.12	Corban's Square	13 A4.14	Cushing Road	12 E2
Coach Hill	40 D3	Corkeran's Quay	12 E3.9	Custom House Quay	25 A2
Coach Street	24 D2.8	Corkscrew Hill	13 C4.10	Custom House Street	25 A2.6
Coakley's Row	27 C2	Corn Market Street	24 E1		
Coal Quay	24 E1	Corporation Buildings	24 E1.26	**D**	
Coburg Street	24 F1	Corran O Gramhna	36 F1.2		
Cockpit Lane	24 E2.4	Corrib Lawn	14 D2	Daffodil Fields	20 D3
Cogan's Cottages	26 D4.8	Corvalley Court	26 E3	Dalton's Avenue	24 E1.13
College Road	23 C3	Cotters Street	24 F3.2	Dean Street	24 D3
College Square	24 D3.7	*Court House Street	24 E2	Deane Street	24 F2.2
College View	11 B4.1	(off Washington St)		Deanrock Avenue	35 B2
College View	23 C3.17	Courtlands	14 F3.1	Deanrock Close	35 C2
College View Terrace	23 C2.2	*Courtney's Avenue	24 E1	Deanrock Cottages	35 B2
Colmcille Avenue	14 D3	(off Roman Street)		Deanrock Terrace	35 C2.7
Comeragh Park	13 A3	Courtown Drive	11 A4.2	*Deanrock Villas	35 B2
Commons Road	3 A4	Courtown Park	11 A4.1	(off Deanrock Cottages)	
Commons Road	12 E2	Cove Street	24 E3	Deanwood Avenue	35 C2
Congress Road	24 F4	*Coyle Square	24 E3	Deanwood Place	35 C2.3
Connaught Avenue	23 C3	(off Evergreen Street)		Deerpark	24 E4
*Connaught Place	24 F1	Crab Lane	26 D3	Deerpark Court	24 E4.2
(on Wellington Road)		Crane Lane	24 F2.14	Deerpark Mews	24 F4.4
Connell Street	24 F2.15	Cranford Pines	31 B1	Deerpark Road	24 E4
Connolly Green	36 D2	Crawford Mews	24 D3.9	Delaney Park	12 F2
Connolly Park	36 D2	Crestfield Downs	8 D2	Delfern Grove	39 B4
				Delford Drive	39 A2

STREET NAME	PAGE / GRID REF	STREET NAME	PAGE / GRID REF	STREET NAME	PAGE / GRID REF
Delwood Grove	27 D3	Dunloe	12 E3.5	Elm Grove	38 D3
*Derrynane Place (on St Anne's Park)	36 F1	Dunmahon	37 C2	Elm Grove Park	13 C3.7
Derrynane Road	24 F4	Dunmanus Park	11 A4	Elm Park	35 A4
Desmond Square	24 E3	Dunmore Gardens	11 B3	Elm Lawn	18 F4
Devonshire Street	24 F1	Dunmore Lawn	25 C4	Elm Park	25 A3.6
Devonshire Street W.	24 D1.29	Dunnycove Crescent	11 B3.1	Elm Road	35 C1
Dierville	12 D1.7	Dunraven Downs	25 B3	Elmvale	35 B3
Dominick Street	24 E1	Dunville Crescent	34 D3.2	Elmvale Avenue	35 A3
Don Bastible Court	35 C2.8	Dunville Estate	34 D3	Elmvale Close	35 B3
Donnybrook	46 F1	Dunville Villas	34 D3.1	Elmvale Court	35 A3
Donnybrook Cottages	46 D1.6	Dyke Parade	24 D2	Elmwood	24 F1.6
Donnybrook Drive	38 D4.1			Elmwood Grove	12 D1.3
Donnybrook Hill	38 D4	**E**		Elton Lawn	33 C1
Donnybrook Terrace	38 D4.7	Earlwood Estate	35 C1	Emmet Place	12 E4.11
Donovan's Road	23 C3	Eason's Avenue	24 E1.8	Empress Place	25 A1.14
Donscourt	34 F2	Eason's Hill	24 E1	Empress Villas	25 A1.13
Dorgan's Road	23 C4	East Douglas Street	38 D2	*Emyville (on Ballinlough Road)	25 B4
Dosel Drive	37 C4	East View Terrace	24 F3.6	Endsleigh	38 D1
Doughcloyne	43 A1	Eastcliff Terrace	25 A3.11	Endsleigh Park	38 D2
Douglas	38 E3	Eastville	25 A2.4	Ennismore Villas	23 B4.8
Douglas Drive	25 C4	*Ebenezer Terrace (off Sunday's Well Rd.)	23 C2	Erin Terrace	24 F4.3
Douglas Hall Lawn	38 D2	Eden Court	28 D2	Errigal Heights	13 A3
Douglas Hall Mews	38 E1.1	Eden Grove	28 D3	Eugene Drive	37 C4
Douglas Lawn	38 E3	Edenbrook Lawn	8 E4	*Evenus Ville (on Geraldine Place)	25 A2.3
Douglas Road	25 B4	Edward Walsh Road	35 C2	Evergreen Buildings	24 E3.16
Douglas Street	24 F3	Egerton Villas	13 A4.12	Evergreen Road	24 F4
Douglas Terrace	25 B4.10	Eglantine Park	37 C1	Evergreen Street	24 E3
Doyle Road	24 F4	Eglinton Place	23 C3.8	Evergreen Villas	24 F4.12
Drawbridge Street	24 F2.4	Eglinton Street	25 A2	*Everleigh Villas (on Blackrock Road)	25 C3
Drews Terrace	24 F3.9	*Elbow Lane (off Cook Street)	24 F2	Exchange Street	24 E1.22
Drinan Street	24 E3	Eileen Villas	23 C4.16	**F**	
Dryden Place	25 B4.9	*Elder Wood (on College Road)	23 C3	*Factory Lane (Gerald Griffin Avenue)	12 E4
Dryden Terrace	25 B4.8	Eldred Terrace	25 B4.13	Factory Lane	27 B2.1
Dublin Hill Lower	12 F2	*Electric Terrace (on Eastville)	25 A2.4	Fair Hill	11 C2
Dublin Hill Middle	12 F1	Elizabeth Place	25 A3.13	Fair Hill	12 D3
Dublin Hill Upper	4 F4	Elizabeth Terrace	25 A2.9	Fair Hill Drive	11 C1
Dublin Pike	5 A3	Elm Bank	25 B4.7	Fair Hill Upper	11 C2
Dublin Street	12 F3	Elm Close	37 C1.1	*Fair Hill Villas (off Fair Hill)	12 D3
Dunbar Street	24 F3	Elm Close	28 D3	Fair Street	24 E1
Dundanion	27 A2	Elm Court	37 C4	Fairfield Avenue	12 D2
Dundanion Court	27 A2.4	Elm Drive	37 C4		
Dundanion Road	26 F3	Elm Grove	25 C4.2		
Dundanion Terrace	27 A2.7				
Dunedin	23 C3.11				
Dunedin	25 C4.4				

STREET NAME	PAGE / GRID REF	STREET NAME	PAGE / GRID REF	STREET NAME	PAGE / GRID REF
Fairfield Crescent	12 D2.1	Ferry Lane	24 E1.2	Friars Walk Terrace	24 E4.4
Fairfield Green	12 D2	Ferry Walk	23 B2	Friary Gardens	24 E4
Fairfield Road	12 D2	Firgrove Avenue	34 E2	*Friary Mews	24 E4
Fairfield Square	11 C2.1	Firgrove Crescent	34 E2.1	(on Friary Gardens)	
Fairhill Heights	11 C2.3	Firgrove Drive	34 E2	Fullers Place	24 D3.10
Fairview	11 C2.2	Firgrove Gardens	34 E2	Fullers Road	24 D3
Fairville	24 D3.13	Firgrove Lawn	34 E1		
Fairwinds	34 D2	Firgrove Park	34 E1	G	
Fairy Ville Lawn	36 D1	Firmount Avenue	26 A4		
Falcon Hill	14 D4	Firview	34 E2.6	Gabriel Terrace	24 E4
Fany's Road	7 A3	Fitton Street East	24 F2.17	Galway's Lane	38 D3
Farleigh Place	13 B4.1	Fitz's Boreen	12 D1	Gaol Walk	23 C3
Farnmore	13 A4.17	Fitzgerald Place	25 A3.2	Gardiner's Hill	13 B4
Farran Cleary Place	12 F3.3	Flaherty's Lane	26 D4.2	Gardiner's Hill Avenue	13 B4.11
Farranferris Avenue	12 D3	Flora View	25 A3.4	Garrane Lane	34 E2
Farranferris Court	12 E3.16	Foley's Row	12 E3.1	Garravagh	17 B2
Farranferris Crescent	12 D2.2	Forest Park	8 F2	Gartan Park	38 E3
Farranferris Green	12 D2	Forest Ridge	35 A4	Gas Works Road	25 A2
Farranferris Park	12 D3.2	Forest Ridge Crescent	35 A4	Gawsworth	19 C1
Farranferris Place	12 D2	Forge Hill	36 D4	Gearneys Boreen	11 C1
Farranlea Grove	22 F3	Fort Street	24 E3	George's Quay	24 F2
Farranlea Park	22 F3	Fota Lawn	11 B4	Gerald Griffin Avenue	12 E4
Farranlea Road	22 F3	Foxford Avenue	34 D2.1	Gerald Griffin Street	12 E4
Farranree	12 E2	Foyle Avenue	11 A4.4	Geraldine Place	25 A2.3
Farren Street	12 E4.3	Fr. Rogers Park	12 E1	Gibraltar Terrace	25 B1.9
Farren's Quay	24 E1.21	Francis Street	24 D1.28	*Gillabbey Court	24 D3
Father Dominic Place	36 D1.4	Francis Street	24 E1.27	(off St Finbarr's Rd)	
Father Dominic Road	36 D1	*Franconia	24 F4	Gillabbey Park	24 D3.1
Father Mathew Quay	24 F2	(on Evergreen Road)		Gillabbey Terrace	24 D3.5
Father Mathew Road	24 F4	Frankfield	36 F4	*Gillabbey Mews	23 C3
Father O'flynn Place	24 D1.2	Frankfield Road	36 F4	(off Connaught Avenue)	
Faulkner's Lane	24 F2.3	*Frankfield Terrace	24 F4	Gillabbey Street	24 D3
*Fern Cliff Villas	13 A4	(on Summer Hill South)		Glandore Avenue	27 A2.2
(on Bellvue Park)		Frankfield View	13 B4.13	Glandore Park	23 B1.2
*Fern Villas	24 D2	Frankfield Villas	24 F3.13	Glandore Villas	27 A2.6
(off Sheares Street)		*Fredaville	23 C3	Glanmire	16 E1
Ferndale Villas	24 D4.8	(on Highfield Avenue)		Glanmire Court	16 D1
Ferney Close	27 C3.2	Fremont Drive	34 D1	Glanmire Road	15 C2
Ferney Grove	27 C2	French Church Street	24 E2.17	Glanmire Road Middle	13 B4
Ferney Road	27 C2	Frenche's Quay	24 E3.19	Glanmire Road Middle	14 E4
Fernhurst Place	23 B3.19	Frenche's Villas	12 D4	Glanmire View	8 D4
Fernhurst Terrace	23 B4.5	Friar Street	24 E3	Glanmire Wood	8 D4
Fernhurst View	23 B4.9	Friar's Avenue	24 D1.23	Glasheen	35 B1
Fernhurst Villas	23 B3.18	Friars Court	36 E2.3	Glasheen Park	23 B4
Fernside Villas	24 F4.9	Friars Road	24 F4	Glasheen Road	23 C4
Fernwood	25 B4.15	Friars Walk	24 E4	Glen View	37 B1.3
				Glen Avenue	12 F3

STREET NAME	PAGE / GRID REF	STREET NAME	PAGE / GRID REF	STREET NAME	PAGE / GRID REF
Glen Avenue	13 A3	Glincool Rise	31 B1	*Grenville Villas (off Grenville Place)	24 D2
Glen Ryan Road	24 D1	Glincool Villas	31 B1	Greystones	20 D4
Glen View	13 C3.5	Golden Villa Terrace	12 E3	Grosvenor Mews	38 D3.1
Glenamoy Lawn	14 E2	Goldsmith's Avenue	12 F4.4	Grosvenor Place	25 A1.9
Glenanaar	25 B3.4	Gordon Terrace	24 F1.5	*Gugan Barra (off Abbey Street)	24 E3
Glenarden	35 A1.2	Gordon's Hill	13 C3	Gurranabraher	11 B4
Glenarm	25 B3.13	Gould's Street	24 D4	Gurranabraher Avenue	24 E1
Glencairn Park	34 D1	Goulden's Place	26 D3.1	Gurranabraher Road	11 C4
Glencoo Gardens	26 D4.7	Grafton Street	24 E2.6	Gweedore Avenue	14 D2
Glencoo Lawn	26 D4	Grand Parade	24 E2		
Glencoo Park	26 D4.1	Grand View Place	13 B3.8	**H**	
Glencree Crescent	14 E2	Grand View Terrace	25 B3.11	Hackett's Terrace	25 B1.6
Glencurrig	37 C3	Grange	45 B1	Haig Gardens	25 B3.1
Glendale Avenue	35 B1.2	Grange Avenue	38 D4	Halcon Drive	14 F4
Glendale Drive	35 B1	Grange Cottages	45 B1	Halcyon Villas	23 C4.15
Glendale Grove	35 B1	Grange Erin	37 C4	Half Moon Lane	37 A1
Glendale Road	35 B1.3	Grange Mews	37 C4	Half Moon Street	24 E1.14
Glendale Walk	35 B1.5	Grange Road	37 C4	Halldene Avenue	33 C3
Glendalough Park	35 C1	Grange Road	44 F1	Halldene Drive	33 C3
Glendower Court	19 C4	Grange Terrace	38 D4.5	Halldene Gardens	33 B3
Glengarriff Road	12 D3	Grange Vale	45 C1	Halldene Grove	33 B3
Glenheights Park	13 A1.4	Grange Vale Court	45 C1.1	Halldene Lawn	33 C3
Glenheights Road	13 A1	Grange Way	45 C1	Halldene Villas	33 C3
Glenmount	13 A3.1	Grange Wood Court	37 C4	Halldene Way	33 C3
Glenryan Mews	24 D1.22	Grattan Street	24 D1	Hanover Place	24 E2.11
Glenside	45 C1	Grattan's Hill	25 B1.12	Hanover Street	24 E2
Glenthorn Avenue	12 F1.1	Grattan's Hill Lower	25 B1.4	*Hansborough Place (on Belgrave Avenue)	24 F1.4
Glenthorn Drive	13 A1	Gray's Lane	24 E1.23	Harbour View Road	11 B4
Glenthorn Mews	13 A1.3	Great William O'Brien St.	12 E4	Harbour View Road	22 F1
Glenthorn Park	13 A1.2	*Green Field Lane (off Abbey Street)	24 E3	*Harbour View Tce (on Summer Hill)	25 A1
Glenthorn Road	13 A1	Green Lawn	36 F1	Hardwick Street	24 F1.7
Glenthorn Villas	13 B4.32	Green Park	35 A1	Harley Court	35 A3.3
Glenthorn Way	13 A1.1	Green Street	24 D3	Harley's Street	24 F1.2
*Glenties (off Glen Avenue)	12 F3	Greenfield	30 D3	Harrington Place	13 B4.6
Glenview	45 C1	Greenfields	22 D4	Harrington Row	13 B4.7
Glenview Terrace	13 B3.5	Greenhills Court	37 B2	Harrington Square	13 B4.9
Glenview Place	13 B4.35	Greenhills Estate	37 B2	Hartland's Avenue	23 C4
Glenview Villas	12 E2.7	Greenmount Avenue	24 D3	Hartland's Road	23 C4
Glenwood Drive	12 D1.1	Greenmount Buildings	24 D3.4	Hattons Alley Lane	12 E3.8
Glincool	31 A1	Greenmount Crescent	24 D3	Hawke's Road	34 D2
Glincool Crescent	31 B1	Greenmount Place	24 D3.3	Hawthorn Avenue	20 D4
Glincool Gardens	31 B1	Greenmount Villas	24 D4.10	Hawthorn Estate	12 F1.2
Glincool Grove	31 B1	Greenwood Estate	35 C3		
Glincool Lawn	31 A1	Gregg Road	24 D3		
Glincool Park	31 A1	Grenville Place	24 D2		

STREET NAME	PAGE / GRID REF	STREET NAME	PAGE / GRID REF	STREET NAME	PAGE / GRID REF
Hawthorn Mews	12 F1	*Hillsboro Place	25 A3	Inchera Close	28 D4
*Hawthorne Place	23 C3	(on Old Blackrock Road)		Inchera Drive	28 D4
(on College Road)		Hillside	45 C1	Inchera Estuary	28 D4
Hawthorne Villas	37 A1.1	Hillside Avenue	35 C1.1	Inchera Lawn	28 D4
Hazel Road	35 C2	Hillside Drive	35 C1	Inchera Park	28 D4
Hazelville	12 D1.8	Hillside Grove	35 C1.2	Inchvale Avenue	38 D4
Hazelwood Avenue	8 D2	Hillside Lawn	35 C1.3	Inchvale Close	38 D4
Hazelwood Close	8 E2	Hillside Road	35 B1	Inchvale Drive	38 D4
Hazelwood Court	8 D2	Hillview Drive	12 D1	Inchvale Lane	37 C3
Hazelwood Drive	8 D2	Hillview Estate	36 E2	Inchvale Park	38 D4
Hazelwood Gardens	8 D2	Hillview Terrace	37 B1.4	Inchvale Road	37 C4
Hazelwood Grove	31 A1	Hilton	20 F3	Industry Place	24 E3.5
Hazelwood Grove	36 E4	Hodders Lane	12 E4.17	Industry Street	24 E3
Hazelwood Way	8 D2	Hodders Villas	18 E4	Infirmary Road	24 F3
Heath Centre	18 E4	Holly Hill	10 F3	Inis Eoghin	14 E3
Heatherton	37 B1	*Holly Hill View	23 C4	Inniscarra	20 D4
*Hegarty's Square	24 D1.12	(on Magazine Road)		Inniscarra Road	12 D4
(off Nicholas Well Lane)		Holly Road	30 F1	Inniscarrig Terrace	24 D2.10
Henry Street	24 D2	Hollygarth	46 D2	Innisfail	23 C4.14
Herbert Park	13 B4	Hollyhill Road	10 F4	Innishannon Road	12 D4
Herbert Park Lawn	13 B4.28	Hollymount	22 F1	Innishmore	18 E4
Hettyfield	38 D1	Hollymount	22 D2	Innishmore Court	18 E4
Hettyfield Mews	38 D1.1	Hollyville	23 A1	Innishmore Drive	18 E4
Hettyfield Park	38 D1	Hollyville	36 F1.1	Innishmore Grove	18 E4
Hettyfields Downs	26 F4.2	Hollyville	45 B1	Innishmore Lawn	18 E4
*Heyland's Lane	12 E3.20	Hollyville Mews	45 B1.1	Innishmore Park	18 E3
(Blackpool Bridge)		Hollywood Estate	22 F1	Innishmore Square	18 E3
Hibernian Buildings	25 A2.2	Holmwood Terrace	25 A3.10	Iona Green	14 E3
Hibernian Road	25 A3	*Home Ville Terrace	23 B2	Iona Park	14 D3
High Street	24 F3	(off Sunday's Well Rd)		Iona Place	14 E3
Highfield Avenue	23 C3	Homeville	23 C4.13	Iona Road	14 D3
Highfield Lawn	22 E4	*Homeville Place	23 C3	Island View	28 D3.4
Highfield West	23 B3	(off Western Road)		Island Way	30 F1
Hill Grove Lane	12 E4.9	Honan Mews	24 D3.8	Ivy Circle	30 F1
*Hill Lane	24 E1	Hop Island	40 F2		
(off Popes Quay)		Horgan's Buildings	23 C3.18	**J**	
*Hill Lane	24 E1	Horgan's Quay	25 A1		
(off Dominick Street)		Hostel Complex	10 F4.2	James Connolly Place	46 D1.2
Hill View Villas	13 B4.17	Hyde Park	23 A2	James Square	24 E3.7
Hillcourt	46 D1			*James Street	24 D2.4
Hillcrest Avenue	23 A1	**I**		(off Anne Street)	
Hillcrest Close	23 A1			Jamesville	23 C2.4
Hillcrest Drive	23 A1	*Idaville	24 D3	Jamesville	26 E2.5
Hillcrest Rise	23 A1	(on Sharman Crawford St.)		Janeville	26 D3
Hillcrest View	23 A1	Ilen Court	35 B2.2	*Janeville Terrace	23 A2
Hillgrove Lawn	37 C2	Illen Villas	23 B2.2	(off Sundays Well Road)	
		*Imaal	12 F3		
		(off Glen Avenue)			

STREET NAME	PAGE / GRID REF	STREET NAME	PAGE / GRID REF	STREET NAME	PAGE / GRID REF
Jessie Ville	24 F4.8	Killeenreendowney Ave.	36 D2	Laburnum Lawn	22 F4
Joe Murphy Road	36 D1	Killiney Heights	11 A4	Laburnum Park	34 F1
John F. Connelly Road	11 C2	Killingley Terrace	24 F4.5	Lackenshoneen	19 A1
John Philpott-Curran St.	24 E1.7	Kilmore Heights	11 A4	Lady's Well Hill	12 F4.5
John Redmond Street	24 E1	Kilmore Road Lower	11 B3	*Lady's Well Place	12 E4
John Street	24 E1	Kilmorna Heights	5 A4	(off Leitrim Street)	
*John Street Little	24 E1	Kiln Road	3 A4	Laffan's Court	12 F2.2
(off John Street)		Kilnap Green	12 D2.6	Lagan Grove	14 E2
John Street Upper	24 E1	Kilnap Place	12 D2	Lake Lawn	38 D1
*Jubilee Villas	24 F3	Kiltegan Crescent	39 A2	Lakeland Avenue	27 C3
(on Dunbar Street)		Kiltegan Lawn	38 F2	Lakeland Crescent	27 C3
		Kimberley Villas	13 A4.13	Lakeview Lawn	28 D2.1
K		King's Terrace	25 A1.11	Lancaster Quay	24 D2
Kearney's Avenue	12 D4.6	Kingsford Park	37 B4	Landsborough	47 C1
Keeffe Street	24 F2.18	Kingslea	38 D4	Landsborough Avenue	47 C2
Kelleher's Buildings	13 B3.1	Kingston Avenue	25 A2.5	Landsborough Close	47 C2
Kempton Park	13 B1	Kinloch Court	22 F4.5	Landsborough Court	47 C2
Kenley	37 C4	Kinsale Cottages	24 F4.6	Landsborough Crescent	47 C1
Kenley Avenue	22 D4	Kinsale Road	36 F2	Landsborough Gardens	47 C1
Kenley Circle	34 E1.2	Kinvara	5 A4	Landsborough Park	47 C2
Kenley Close	22 D4	Knapp's Square	24 E1.1	Landscape Park	36 D1
Kenley Crescent	34 D1	Knights Court	14 D3.4	*Landscape Terrace	23 C1
Kenley Drive	22 D4	Knockfree Avenue	11 C4	(off Sunday's Well Ave)	
Kenley Heights	34 D1	*Knockluan	13 B4	Landscape Terrace	23 C4.20
Kenley Road	22 D4	(on Ballyhooly New Road)		*Langford Place	24 F3
Kennedy Quay	25 B2	Knocknaheeny	11 A3	(off Langford Row)	
*Keoghan's Lane	24 D1	Knocknaheeny Avenue	11 B4	Langford Row	24 F3
(off Blarney Street)		Knockpogue Avenue	12 D2	Langford Terrace	24 F3.12
*Keohane's Lane	24 D1	Knockpogue Park	12 D3.1	Lansdowne Court	12 F4.7
(off Glen Ryan Road)		*Knockrea	25 C3	Lansdowne Terrace	12 F4.11
Kerry Lawn	14 E3.1	(on Blackrock Road)		Lapp's Quay	24 F2
Kerry Road	14 E3	Knockrea Drive	25 B4.5	Lapps Court	23 C4.6
Kerryhall Road	12 D4	Knockrea Gardens	25 B4.2	Larchfield	11 C1
Kevington Close	37 C4.1	Knockrea Lawn	25 B4.18	Laurel Bank	22 E4
Keysers Hill	24 E3.2	Knockrea Mews	25 B4.4	Laurel Court	34 E2.4
Kift's Lane	24 E2.9	Knockrea Park	25 B4	Laurel Grove	34 E2
Kilbarry Cottages	12 F1	Knockrea Terrace	25 A3.9	Laurel Hurst	23 C3.13
Kilbarry Place	12 E2	*Knockrea Villas	25 A3.5	Laurel Park	26 D4.3
Kilbrack Lawn	27 A4	(off Carrig View Tce)		Laurel Ridge	23 A1
Kilcolman Lawn	37 A1.2	Kyle Street	24 E1	Laurel Villas	23 B3.8
Kilcrea Park	23 B4	Kyrl's Quay	24 E1	Laurelmount	23 C4.7
Kilcully	5 A2	Kyrl's Street	24 E1.12	Laurelville Cottages	26 D4.9
Kilkieran Close	11 A4.3			Laurelwood	25 A4.9
Killala Gardens	11 B4	**L**		Lavitt's Quay	24 E1
Killeen's Green	12 D2.5	Laburnum Drive	34 F1	Leafdale	35 C1
Killeen's Place	12 D2	Laburnum Grove	12 D1.5	Leamlara Close	35 B2.1

STREET NAME	PAGE / GRID REF	STREET NAME	PAGE / GRID REF	STREET NAME	PAGE / GRID REF
Leary's Place	24 D3[6]	Little Market Street	24 E1[25]	Lynbrook	35 A1
Lee Road	22 F2	Little William Street	24 F1[12]	Lynch's Street	24 D2
Lee View	23 A2[5]	*Lloyd's Lane	24 E1	Lyndon Crescent	46 E2[1]
*Lee View Place	23 B2	(off John Redmond Street)			
(off Sunday's Well Road)		Long Range	19 B3		

M

STREET NAME	PAGE / GRID REF	STREET NAME	PAGE / GRID REF	STREET NAME	PAGE / GRID REF
*Lee View Terrace	24 D1	Loreto Park	37 B1	MacCurtain Villas	24 D3
(off Blarney Street)		Loretto Park	36 E1	MacSwiney's Villas	24 D1[1]
*Lee's Terrace	25 B4	Loretto Ville	23 C4[11]	Madden's Buildings	12 E3[12]
(Ballinlough Road)		Lota	15 C4	Magazine Road	23 C4
Leesdale	34 D1	*Lota·View	27 A2	Magdala Terrace	13 B4[26]
Leesdale Court	19 B3	(on Blackrock Road)		Maglin	31 B3
Leesdale Drive	19 B4	Lotabeg Estate	14 F3	Maglin Grove	35 B2[4]
Leesdale Estate	19 B3	Lotabeg Green	15 A3[1]	Maglin Drive	31 A1
Leesdale Grove	19 B3	Lotabeg Road Upper	14 F3	Maglin Road	31 A1
Leecourt	19 B3	Lotabeg Terrace	14 F3	Maglin Vale	31 B1
Leeview	19 B3	Lotamore Avenue	15 A2	Maglin View	31 A1
Leitrim Street	12 E4	Lotamore Close	15 A2	Magnolia Terrace	25 B1[10]
Leycester's Lane	13 C4[8]	Lotamore Crescent	15 A2	Mahon	27 C3
Liam Healy Road	12 D3	Lotamore Drive	15 A2	Mahon Avenue	38 D2
Liam Lynch Park	35 A1	Lotamore Grove	15 A2	Mahon Crescent	27 C3
*Libertas Villas	27 A2	Lotamore Lawn	15 A2	Mahon Drive	27 C3
(on Blackrock Road)		Lotamore Park	15 A2	Mahon Park	27 C3
Liberty Street	24 E2	Lough Park	24 D4	Mahon Terrace	27 B2[2]
Liffey Park	14 E2	Lough Road	24 D4	Mahony's Avenue	25 B1
Lima Lawn	23 B4	Lough View Terrace	23 C4[2]	Mahony's Place	24 E1[4]
Lime Trees Road	38 F3	Lough Villas	24 D4[1]	Mahony's Square	12 E3[18]
Lime Trees Road East	39 A3	Loughmahon Avenue	28 D3[1]	Main Street	19 A4
Limes Avenue	27 C2[2]	Loughmahon Close	27 C3[3]	Maire Place	24 F3[11]
Limewood Grove	12 D2	Loughmahon Court	27 C3[5]	Maiville Terrace	24 F4[13]
Linaro Avenue	23 A4[1]	Loughmahon Drive	28 D3[2]	Mallow Road	4 D4
Lincoln's Place	25 B1[15]	Loughmahon Road	28 D3	Mangerton Close	12 F3
Linden Avenue	26 F4	Lover's Walk	26 D1	Manor Avenue	40 D3
Lisadell	39 A4	Lovers Walk	12 E3	Manor Circle	40 D3
*Lisaniska	23 C3	*Lower Barrack View	12 E4[10]	Manor Close	40 D3
(on Western Road)		(off Church Avenue)		Manor Crescent	40 D3
Lisieux Park	23 B4	Lower Friars Walk	36 E1	Manor Dene	40 D3
Lislee Road	38 F3	Lower Glanmire Road	15 C4	Manor Downs	40 E3
*Lisnacairn	25 C3	Lower Glanmire Road	25 A1	Manor Drive	40 D3
(off Blackrock Road)		Lower Janemount Tce.	23 C1[7]	Manor Gardens	40 D3
Lisnalee Drive	26 F2	Lower Kensington Rd.	40 D3	Manor Grove	40 D4
*Little Anne Street	24 E2	Lower Killeen's Road	10 E2	Manor Hill	19 C3
(off Washington St)		Lower Killeen's Road	3 B4	Manor Heath	40 D3
*Little Cross Street	24 E2	Lower Mayfield Road	14 F3	Manor Lawn	40 D3
(off Washington St)		Lower View Ville	23 B2[3]	Manor Orchard	40 D4
Little Hanover Street	24 D2[3]	Lucan Place	23 B3[11]	Manor Rise	40 E3
Little Island	28 F1	Lucerne	23 C3[12]	Manor Villas	40 D3

STREET NAME	PAGE / GRID REF	STREET NAME	PAGE / GRID REF	STREET NAME	PAGE / GRID REF
*Mans Lane (off North Mall)	24 D1	Maryborough Heights	39 A4	Merchant Street	24 F2
Maple Lawn	30 F1	Maryborough Hill	38 F3	Merchant's Quay	24 F1
Maple Place	35 C1.4	Maryborough Hill	39 A4	Mercier Park	36 F1
*Marble Hall Close (adj Marble Hall Cotts)	25 B4	Maryville	24 F2.1	Merlyn Lawn	34 E2
		*Maryville (on Mardyke Walk)	23 C2	Merrion Court	13 C4
*Marble Hall Cotts (on Ballinlough Rd)	25 B4	Maryville	24 E4.5	Mervue Crescent	13 B1
		Maryville	26 E2	Mervue Lawn	13 B1
Marble Hall Gardens	25 A4.11	Maryville Court	26 E2.7	Michael Fitzgerald Rd.	36 D2.1
Marble Hall Park	25 A3	Maryville Mews	26 E2.3	*Middle Row (off Sunday's Well Ave.)	23 C1
Marble Hill	26 E3.2	Mathew Place	26 E2.4		
Marble Park	8 E3	Maybury	23 C4.18	Military Road	13 A4
Mardyke Street	24 D2.5	*Maybury Court (on Magazine Road)	23 C4	Mill Range	19 B3
*Mardyke Villas (on Mardyke Walk)	23 C2			Mill Road	25 B2
		Mayfield	14 E3	*Mill Row (on Friars Walk)	24 E4
Mardyke Walk	23 C2	Mayfield Park	14 D3.5		
Margaret Street	24 F3.3	Maylor Street	24 F2	Millbrook	38 E4.2
Marguerita Villas	24 E3.18	Maymount	24 D1.15	Millbrook Lawn	24 E4.3
Maria Villas	24 D3.17	Maymount	24 E3.11	Millerd Street	24 D1
Marian Close	12 F1.3	Maymount Villas	13 C3.4	Millfield Cottages	12 F1.5
Marian Park	26 A3	McCurtain Street	24 F1	Millfield Lawn	12 F1
Marian Park	12 F1	McCurtain's Villas	24 D3	Millfield Terrace	12 F1.4
Marian Park	24 D4	McDonagh Road	36 D2	Millford	35 B4
Marian Place	23 B3.1	McGrath Park	26 A4	Millview Cottages	12 E3.19
Marian Terrace	45 B1	Meade Street	24 E2.14	Minerva Terrace	24 D3.12
Marian Ville	13 A4.8	Meadow Park	13 B2	Model Cottages	23 C1.2
Marie Ville	36 D2.2	Meadow Park Avenue	13 B2	Model Farm Road	20 E4
Marina Park	25 B2	Meadow Park Close	13 B2.1	Model Farm Road	22 F3
Marina Walk	25 B2	Meadow Park Drive	13 C1.1	*Model Villas (on Gardiners Hill)	13 B4
Marina Terrace	25 A2.8	Meadow Park Grove	13 B2.2		
*Marina View (on Victoria Road)	25 A2	Meadow Park Lawn	13 B1	Monahan's Road	25 B2
		Meadow Park Road	13 B2	Monastery Road	40 E4
*Marina Villas (adj to Geraldine Place)	25 A2.3	Meadowbrook Estate	8 D3	Monaville	23 C4.21
		Meadowgrove Estate	26 B3	Monerea Terrace	25 A2.7
Marina Walk	25 B2	Meelick Park	13 B1	Moneyflugh	17 A1
*Market Lane (off St Patrick's Street)	24 E2	Melbourn Avenue	34 D2	Montenotte	13 C4
		Melbourn Close	46 E2.2	Montenotte Grove	13 C3.1
Markland Woods	39 A4	Melbourn Court	21 C4	Montenotte Road	13 C4
Marlborough Street	24 F2	Melbourn Mews	34 D1.2	*Montenotte View (adj to Eastville)	25 A2.4
Mary Aikenhead Place	24 D1	Melbourn Road	34 D1		
Mary Street	24 E3	*Melville Terrace (on Bellvue Park)	13 A4	Montford Park	23 B3.2
Mary Ville Cottages	13 B4.12			Montpellier Place	25 A1.10
*Mary's Lane (off John Street)	24 E1	Menloe Gardens	26 F2	Montpellier Road	46 E2
		Menloe Park	26 F2	Moore Street	24 D2.1
Maryborough Avenue	38 F3	Mentone Place	23 C2.1	*Moorfield Tce (on South Douglas Road)	37 A1
Maryborough Court	39 A4	*Mentone Villas (off Sunday's Well Rd)	23 C2		

STREET NAME	PAGE / GRID REF	STREET NAME	PAGE / GRID REF	STREET NAME	PAGE / GRID REF
Morgan Street	24 F2	Murmont Crescent	14 D3	North Ring Road	14 F4
Morningside	24 F4.10	Murmont Drive	13 C3.2	Norwood Court	40 D3
Morrison's Quay	24 F2	Murmont Grove	14 D3.2	Nun's Walk	24 D4
*Morton Villas	24 F3.4	Murmont Lawn	13 C3	Nursery Drive	25 C4
(off Needham Place)		Murmont Park	14 D3	Nutley Avenue	27 C2
*Motor Villas	12 F4	Murmont Road	14 D3	Nutley Road	27 C2
(on Popes Road)		Murmont Villas	13 C3.6		
Mount Agnes Road	11 C3	Murphy's Gardens	24 F4.2	O	
*Mount Brandon	13 B4	Muskerry Estate	18 F4		
(on Gardiners Hill)		*Muskerry Villas	24 D2	O'Connell Avenue	24 F4
Mount Brosna	14 D3	(off Lancaster Quay)		O'Connell Crescent	24 F4.1
Mount Carmel	22 F4.4	Mutton Lane	24 E2.18	*O'Connell Place	12 E4
Mount Carmel Road	24 E3	Myrtle Hill Terrace	26 D1.1	(off Watercourse Road)	
Mount Eden	34 E1	Myrtle Ville	25 A3.12	O'Connell Square	24 E1.6
Mount Eden Rise	23 C1.4			O'Connell Street	12 E4.5
Mount Eden Road	23 C1	N		O'Connor Ville	24 E3
Mount Eden Terrace	23 C1.5			O'Donovan Rossa Road	23 C3
Mount Erne	14 E2	Nano Nagle Bridge	24 E2.22	Oakdale	23 A1
Mount Farran	12 F3	Nano Nagle Place	24 F3.10	Oakdeane	27 B3
Mount Farran Place	12 F3.1	Nash's Boreen	11 B2	Oakfield Lawn	25 C4
Mount Nebo Avenue	23 C1	*Nashville Terrace	23 C3	Oakgrove	33 C2.1
Mount Ovel	39 B3	(on Highfield Avenue)		Oaklands	31 A1
Mount Pleasant Avenue	24 E4	Needham Place	24 F3.4	Oaklee	20 F3
Mount Pleasant Road	24 E4	Nelson Terrace	25 B1.13	Oakpark	13 C2
Mount Prospect	23 A2.4	*Nessan Place	24 D3	Oakview	37 C4
Mount Prospect	23 C4.19	(on Bandon Road)		Oakview Drive	37 C4
Mount Sion Road	24 E3	New Inn	15 B1	Oakview Lawn	37 C4
Mount St Joseph's View	23 C3.7	New Mallow Road	3 B4	Oakville Drive	11 C1
Mount Verdon Terrace	25 A1.20	New Road	13 B3	Old Blackrock Road	25 A3
Mount Vernon Crescent	37 C3	Newenham Drive	38 F3	Old Cliff	26 F4.4
Mount Vernon Terrace	13 A4.1	*Newenham Place	24 F3	Old Friary Place	24 E1.19
Mount Vernon View	13 A4.11	(off Infirmary Road)		Old Market Place	24 D1
*Mount View Terrace	23 C2	Newlyn Vale	39 B3	*Old Post Office Lane	24 E3
(Sunday's Well Road)		Newton Court	45 B1	(off Sth Main St)	
Mount View Terrace	13 B4.15	Nicholas Church Lane	24 E3.14	Old Station Road	25 A2.11
Mountain View	25 A1.17	Nicholas Hill	24 D1.19	Old Whitechurch Road	4 E4
Mountpleasant	23 C3.14	Nicholas Lane	24 D1.7	Oliver Plunkett St.	24 E2
Mourne Avenue	13 A3	Nicholas Street	24 F3	Oliver Plunkett St. Lr.	24 F2
*Moylan's Lane	24 E1	Nicholas Well Lane	24 D1.12	Ophelia Place	24 D4.6
(off John Redmond St)		Ninety Eight Street	24 D3	Orchard Close	37 C1.2
*Mulgrave Place	24 E1	Noonan Road	24 D3	Orchard Road	23 A4
(off John Redmond St)		North Abbey Square	24 D1.9	Orrery Road	23 C1
Murmont Avenue	13 C3	North Abbey Street	24 D1.10	Orrery Terrace	11 B4.2
Murmont Circle	13 C3	North Main Street	24 E1	Ossory Place	24 F4.7
Murmont Close	14 D3.1	North Mall	24 D1	Our Lady of Lourdes Pk.	26 D4.4
Murmont Court	14 D3.3	North Monastery Road	12 E4	Owenabue Close	35 B2.6
		North Ring Road	13 A2	Owenacurra Court	35 C2.1

STREET NAME	PAGE / GRID REF
P	
Palace View Place	24 D2.14
Palaceanne Court	37 A1.7
Palaceanne Lawn	37 A1
Palaceanne Villas	37 A1.6
Palmbury	35 C3
Palmbury Orchard	35 B4
Palmgrove	8 E3
Pampas Grove	33 C3.1
Panorama Terrace	24 D1.16
Panorama Terrace Upr.	24 D1.17
Park Avenue	26 E2
Park Court	13 B2
Park Court	11 B1
Park Gate	45 A1
Park Gate Villas	34 F2.6
Park Grove	11 C1
Park Lawn	11 C1
Park Road	30 F1
*Park View	24 F1
(Wellington Road)	
Park View	11 C1
Park View	25 A2.10
*Park View Terrace	24 F1
(on Wellington Road)	
Park Villas	25 B3.12
Park Wood Close	11 C1.1
Parklands	11 C1
Parklands Drive	11 C1
Parklea Court	22 D4
Parkmead Close	11 C1
Parkmoor	24 D1.24
Parknamore	30 E1
Parknamore Heights	30 E1
Parknamore Rise	30 D1
Parkowen	24 F3.5
Parkway Drive	22 D4
Parliament Street	24 F2.20
Parnell Place	24 F2
Parnell Terrace	24 D4.16
Patrick O'Donoghue Pl.	36 D1.3
Patrick Trahy Road	36 D1
Paul Street	24 E1
Paul's Lane	24 E1.24
Pearse Park	38 D4

STREET NAME	PAGE / GRID REF
Pearse Place	36 D1
Pembroke Street	24 F2.22
Penrose's Quay	25 A1
Perrott Avenue	23 C3
Perry Street	24 F1.3
Peter O'Donovan Cres.	19 B4
Peter's Street	24 D2
Phoenix Street	24 F2.13
Pic Du Jer Close	25 C4.3
Pic Du Jer Park	25 C4
*Pinafore Villas	13 A4
(on Military Road)	
Pine Court	27 A4.1
Pine Street	24 F1
Pine Walk	19 A4
Pinecroft	45 C1
Pinewood	34 E2.5
Pinewood	35 A4
Pinewood	25 B4.16
*Pinewood	25 B4
(on Ballinlough Road)	
Pinewood Grove	12 D2
Plas De Barra	12 D4.5
Plas Mac Diarmada	24 E4.1
Plas Ó Ceallachain	12 D4.4
Plas Ó Conghaile	36 E2.1
Plunkett Road	36 D2
Pope's Quay	24 E1
Pope's Road	12 F4
Popham's Road	12 E2
Portney's Lane	24 E2.16
Post Office Lane	27 A2.1
Pouladuff Place	36 D1.5
Pouladuff Road	36 D3
Presentation Avenue	12 D4.7
Presentation Close	11 B4.3
Presentation Place	24 E3
Presentation Road	11 C4
Princes Street	24 E2
Proby's Quay	24 E3
Prospect Place	23 C1.8
Prospect Row	24 D2.7
Prosperity Square	24 E3.4
Prosperous Place	12 F3.2
Q	

STREET NAME	PAGE / GRID REF
Quaker Road	24 F3
*Quarry Lane	24 E1
(off John Redmond Street)	
R	
Raheen	33 A1
Railway Cottages	25 A3.7
Railway Place	25 A4.3
Railway Street	25 A1
Rathcooney Road	6 E4
Rathmore Buildings	12 F4.3
Rathmore Lawn	37 C2
Rathmore Park	12 F4
*Rathmore Place	12 F4
(Richmond Hill)	
Rathmore Road	13 A3
*Rathmore Terrace	12 F4
(Rathmore Park)	
Rathpeacon Road	12 D2
Ravenscourt Avenue	46 D1.3
Ravenscourt Estate	46 E1
Ravensdale Avenue	28 D3
Ravensdale Road	28 D3
*Red Abbey Street	24 E3
(off Mary Street)	
Red Bridge Mews	24 E3.22
Redclyffe Terrace	23 B3.16
Redemption Road	12 E4
Redforge Road	12 F1
Reed's Square	24 E3
Reendowney Place	24 E4
Ravensdale Close	28 D3.3
Rhodaville Estate	37 C1
Richmond	35 A3
Richmond Avenue	13 B4.3
Richmond Estate	25 C3
Richmond Hill	12 F4
Richmond Park	7 C2
*Richmond Terrace	13 B4
(off Gardiners Hill)	
Richmond Wood	7 C2
Ringcroft Avenue	28 D4
Ringcroft View	28 D3
Ringmahon Avenue	27 C2
Ringmahon Close	27 C2.1
Ringmahon Road	27 B3

STREET NAME	PAGE / GRID REF	STREET NAME	PAGE / GRID REF	STREET NAME	PAGE / GRID REF
River Lane	24 D1.18	Roger Casement Park	35 A1	Sandymount Court	12 F4.6
River View	27 B2.4	Roman Street	24 E1	Sandymount Drive	35 B2
Riverbank	33 B3.1	*Roman Walk	24 E1	*Santerem	25 A3
Riverbank	38 D2.1	(off John Redmond Street)		(off Castlegreina Park)	
Riverside Mews	24 D1.21	Rope Walk	23 A2	Sarahville Place	36 D2.3
Riverstown	8 D3	Rope Walk	27 B2	Sarsfield Road	35 A2
Riverview	8 D2	Rose Garth	46 D1	Sarsfield Road	35 A4
Riverview Estate	13 B2	Rose Hill	23 A2.1	*Sarsfield's Terrace	12 F4
Riverview Estate	35 B1	Rose Lawn	35 C2	(on Richmond Hill)	
*Riverview Terrace	25 B1.12	Rosebank	37 B1	Sawmill Lane	24 F3.8
(off Grattan's Hill)		Rosedale Park	34 E3	Sawmill Street	24 F3
Robert Street	24 F2	*Rosefield Terrace	25 A2.5	Scairt Hill	46 D2
*Robertsville	24 E3	(on Kingston Avenue)		School Avenue	23 B4
(on Tower Street)		Rosegreen Avenue	26 F4	School Avenue	12 D4.2
Robin Hill	23 B4.3	Roselawn	24 D4.14	School Place	12 D4.3
Robinscourt	35 B3	Roseneath Villas	13 A4.10	Seamus Quirke Park	26 E4.1
Roche's Buildings	12 F4.2	Rosenheim	23 C4.9	Seminary Buildings	12 E3.13
Rochelle Park	24 B3	Rosepark	37 B1	Seminary Place	12 E2.4
Rochestown	40 E3	*Roserie Gardens	23 C3	Seminary Road	12 E3
Rochestown Rise	39 A3	(off Western Road)		Seminary Villas	12 E3.6
Rochestown Road	39 C3	Roseville	25 B3.8	Seminary Walk	12 E2
*Rock Cottages	24 D1.9	Roseville	25 A4.7	Seven Oaks	45 A1
(North Abbey Square)		Rosewood	19 C4	Shamrock Avenue	38 D4
Rock Cottages	12 E3.17	Roslyn Court	34 D1.5	Shamrock Close	38 D4.2
Rock Lawn Terrace	26 D4.10	Rossa Avenue	21 C4	Shamrock Drive	38 D4.3
*Rock Steps	24 D1	Rossa Avenue	34 D2	Shamrock Drive	19 A4
(off Blarney Street)		Rossalee Close	14 E3	Shamrock Grove	14 E2.1
Rock Villas	24 D1.27	Rossbrook	21 C4	Shamrock Park	37 C4
Rock Villas	23 C3.15	Rowanville	11 C1	Shamrock Place	24 D3.16
Rock Well Lane	24 D1.14	*Rowland's Lane	24 E1	Shamrock Road	38 D4
Rockboro Avenue	25 A3	(off John Redmond St)		Shanakiel Court	23 A1.1
Rockboro Court	25 A3.14	Russell Court	12 E2.6	Shanakiel Lawn	23 B2.6
Rockboro Road	25 A3	Rutland Street	24 F3	Shanakiel Place	23 B2.1
Rockboro Terrace	25 B3.7	Ryan's Buildings	24 D1.26	Shanakiel Place	23 A1.2
Rockcliffe Terrace	26 F2.6			Shanakiel Road	23 A2
Rockcliffe Village	26 F2.4	**S**		*Shanakiel Tce	23 B1
Rockfield	27 A3	Sallybrook	7 C2	(off Strawberry Hill)	
Rockgrove Estate	27 A2.3	*Salmon View Tce	23 C1	Shandon Court	12 F4.9
Rockgrove Square	25 C1.1	(off Sunday's Well Ave)		*Shandon Place	24 E1
Rockgrove Terrace	25 C1.2	Salvador Place	23 B3.3	(off Shandon Street)	
Rockspring	13 B4.29	Sandbrook	35 A3	Shandon Street	24 E1
Rockspring Terrace	13 B4.24	Sandown	37 C4	*Shandon Terrace	12 E4.10
Rockvale	25 C1.3	Sandown Crescent	35 B4	(off Church Avenue)	
Rockview Terrace	13 C4.1	*Sandy Hill Terrace	12 F4	Shandon View Cottages	12 F4.8
Rockwell Terrace	12 E4.18	(Popes Road)		Shannakiel Park	23 A2.3
Rockwood	28 D3	Sandymount Avenue	35 B2	Shannon Lawn	14 E2

STREET NAME	PAGE / GRID REF	STREET NAME	PAGE / GRID REF	STREET NAME	PAGE / GRID REF
Sharman Crawford Street	24 D3	Sorrenta Villas	25 B3.10	St Anthony's Villas	38 D3.4
Sheare's Avenue	23 A4.2	South City Link Road	25 A2	St Brendan's Road	12 E2.3
Sheare's Park	35 A1	South City Link Road	36 F3	*St Bridget's Villa	13 B4
Sheares Street	24 D2	South Douglas Road	37 A1	(Ballyhooly New Rd)	
Sheraton Court	23 C4.5	South Douglas Road	37 C2	St Brigid's Road	24 D1
Ship Street	25 A1	South Gate Bridge	24 E2.21	*St Brigids Street	24 E3
Shournagh Lawn	35 C2.4	South Lodge	38 D1	(off Tower Street)	
Shrewsbury	26 D4	South Lodge Grove	26 D4.6	St Clare's Avenue	23 B4
Shrewsbury Downs	26 D4	South Main Street	24 E2	St Colman's Road	12 E2.2
Shrewsbury Villas	13 A4.18	South Mall	24 F2	St Colmcille Road	11 C4
Sidney Park	24 F1	South Rampart	24 E3.21	St Colomba's Terrace	38 D3.3
Sidney Place	24 F1.10	South Ring Road	37 B3	St Declan's Road	12 D4.9
Sidney Terrace	25 B1.8	South Terrace	24 F3	*St Dominick's Place	24 E1
*Sidneyville	13 A4	South View	25 A4.8	(Dominick Street)	
(on Bellvue Park)		Southbury Road	35 A2	St Dominick's Terrace	24 E3.23
Silver Manor	26 E4	Southern Road	25 A3	*St Dominick's Terrace	24 E3.19
Silver Spring Lane	14 F4	*Southern View Place	24 F3	(Frenche's Qy.)	
Silver Spring Road	14 E3.3	(on High Street)		St Enda's Road	11 C4
Silvercourt	14 F3	Spriggs Road	11 C4	*St Finbar's Place	24 D4
Silverdale Avenue	26 E4	Spring Lane	12 F2	(on Lough Road)	
Silverdale Drive	26 F4.1	*Spring Place	13 B4	St Finbar's Terrace	24 D4.11
Silverdale Grove	26 E4	(on Gardiners Hill)		*St Finbar's View	24 D4
Silverdale Road	26 E4	Springfield Estate	14 E3	(on Lough Road)	
Silverdale Walk	26 E4	Springfield Road	14 E3	St Finbarr's Park	23 C4
Silverheights Avenue	14 F3	Springfort	14 D4	St Finbarr's Place	24 E3.20
Silverheights Drive	14 F3	Springmount	7 C3	St Finbarr's Road	24 D3
Silverheights Road	14 F3	Springmount Close	8 D3	St Finbarr's Street	24 E3.8
Silversprings Court	14 F4	Springmount Drive	8 D3	St Francis Avenue	23 B4
Silversprings Lawn	14 F3	Springmount Place	13 B3.6	St Francis Cottages	12 F2.1
Silverwood	19 A4	Springmount Road	8 D3	St Francis Villas	24 D4.18
*Sion Villas	24 D2	Springview Terrace	12 E2.8	St Gerard Majella Terrace	26 E3.1
(off Sheare's Street)		Spur Hill	35 B4	St Gerard's Place	40 F3
Skehard Road	26 F4	Spur Hill	42 F2	St Helen's Court	23 C4.3
Skehard Road	27 A4	Sraid An Athar Maitiu	24 F2.19	*St James Pl	13 B4
Skiddy's Homes	24 D4.13	St Ann's Road	24 D1	(on Ballyhooly New Rd)	
Skiddy's Homes	35 C2.5	St Ann's Terrace	12 E4.14	St John's	25 B3.14
Sli Gartan	14 E3	St Anne's Drive	13 C4	St John's Mews	24 F3.7
Sliabh Mish Park	36 F1	St Anne's Mews	24 E1.16	St John's Square	12 E4.6
Slighe San Criostoir	13 C4	St Anne's Park	36 F1	St John's Well	11 C1
Smith Street	24 F2	*St Anne's Place	36 F1	St Johns Terrace	13 B4.38
Smithgrove Terrace	13 B4.2	(on St Anne's Park)		St Joseph's Drive	13 C4
Sober Lane	24 E2.23	St Anthony's Road	24 D1	St Joseph's Gardens	34 E2.7
Soho Terrace	23 B2.4	St Anthony's Villas	24 D4.15	St Joseph's Lawn	34 E2
Somerton Drive	26 D4.5	St Augustine Street	24 E2.3	St Joseph's New Road	13 C3.3
Somerton Park	26 D4	St Anyhony's Villas	24 E4.6	St Joseph's Park	14 F2
Somerton Road	25 C4	St Anthony's Villas	13 B3.7	St Joseph's Park	35 C1

STREET NAME	PAGE / GRID REF	STREET NAME	PAGE / GRID REF	STREET NAME	PAGE / GRID REF
St Joseph's Place	25 B3·16	*St Patrick's Tce (off St Mary's Rd)	12 C4	Sunday's Well Avenue	23 C1
St Joseph's Terrace	24 D4·12			Sunday's Well Road	23 A2
St Joseph's Terrace	24 F4·14	*St Patrick's Tce (on Lr Glanmire Rd)	25 A1	Sunday's Well Road	24 D1
St Joseph's Terrace	13 B4·20			Sundrive Park	26 D4
St Joseph's View	8 D3	St Patricks Terrace	38 D3·2	Sunmount	13 A4·16
St Joseph's Villas	13 B4·31	St Paul's Avenue	24 E1	Sunningdale	31 A1
St Joseph's Villas	25 B3·15	St Peter's Avenue	24 E2·5	Sunnyside	23 B3·15
St Kevin's Square	24 E3·15	St Philomena's Road	12 D4·8	Sunnyside	25 C4·1
St Kevin's Street	24 E3	St Rita's Avenue	25 D1	Sunnyside	26 F2·3
*St Kildas (on Western Road)	23 C3	St Rita's Villas	24 E1·18	Sunvalley Drive	12 D4
		*St Stephen's Place (off Stephen Street)	24 E3·6	Sunview Place East	13 B3·3
St Luke's Avenue	25 B1·1			*Sunview Place East (off Ballyhooly New Rd)	13 D4
*St Luke's Place (on Summerhill)	25 A1	St Theresa's Road	24 D1·6		
		St Vincent's Place	24 E1·5	Sunview Terrace	23 C3·5
*St Luke's Villas (Alexandra Road)	13 A4	St Vincent's Street	12 D4	Sunview Terrace	37 A1·4
		*St Vincent's Tce (off St Mary's Rd)	12 C4	Sunview Villas	37 A1·5
St Mary's Avenue	12 D4			Sutton's Buildings	12 F4·1
St Mary's Avenue	12 E4·15	St Vincent's View	24 D2·12	Sweetbriar Grove	20 D4
St Mary's Avenue	13 B3·2	S.S. Peter & Paul's Place	24 E2·2	Sweetbriar Lane	20 D4
St Mary's Place	12 D4·1	Stable Lane	24 F3·1	Sycamore Place	35 C1
St Mary's Place	23 C3·9	Standard's Grove	27 A4·2	*Sydenham (on Belgrave Avenue)	24 F1·4
St Mary's Place	13 B4·23	Starch Hill	1 A4		
St Mary's Road	12 E4	Station Road	19 A4		
*St Mary's Terrace (on Gould's Street)	24 D4	Step Lane	24 E3·13		T
		Stephen Street	24 E3·6	Tara Court	23 B4
*St Mary's Terrace (Wolfe Tone Street)	12 D4	Stockton Close	37 C4	Tara Lawn	35 B1·4
		Stratton Pines	34 E3·1	Temple Gardens	26 F2·2
St Mary's Terrace	13 B4·22	*Straw Hall (off Farren Street)	12 E4·3	Templehill	19 C2
St Mary's Villas	24 D2·13			Temple Hill Lawn	26 E3·5
St Mary's Villas	24 D4·17	Strawberry Hill	23 B1	Temple Lawn	26 D3·3
St Mary's Villas	12 F4·10	Stream Hill	13 B4·34	*Temple Place (on Blackrock Road)	25 C3
St Michael's Road	12 E2·1	*Strowan Villas (on Gardiners Hill)	13 B4		
*St Michael's Tce (on Blackrock Road)	27 A2			Temple Vale	26 F3
		Sullivans Quay	24 E2	Templeacre Avenue	11 C4
St Michaels Lawn	27 C4	Summerhill	25 A1	*Terdolanto (on Lough Road)	24 D4
St Nessan Street	24 E3·9	Summerhill Place	25 A1·18		
St Nicholas Square	24 D1·25	Summer Hill South	24 F4	Terence McSweeny Quay	24 F2·23
St Patrick's Hill	24 F1	Summerhill Terrace	25 A1·15	The Acre	36 D2·4
St Patrick's Place	24 F1·9	Summerstown Avenue	35 A2·1	The Acres	26 E1·1
St Patrick's Presbytery	25 A1·12	Summerstown Drive	35 A2	The Avenue	47 B2
St Patrick's Quay	24 F1	Summerstown Grove	35 A2	The Belfry	22 F4·3
St Patrick's Road	24 E4	Summerstown Road	35 A2	The Circle	47 B1
St Patrick's Street	24 E2	Sun Nook Park	25 B3·3	The Cottages	36 E2·2
*St Patrick's Tce (on Magazine Rd)	23 B4	Sunday School Lane	12 E3·15	The Cottages	26 E2·2
		Sunday's Well	23 B2	The Cottages	26 F2·1
*St Patrick's Tce (on Pouladuff Rd)	36 D3			The Crescent	47 B2

STREET NAME	PAGE / GRID REF
The Crescent	13 B4.4
The Crescent	25 A4.2
The Crescent	26 F3
The Drive	47 B1
The Fairways	46 E2
The Green	46 E2
The Grove	23 A2
The Grove	23 A3
The Grove	22 D4
The Grove	47 B1
The Headlands	35 A3
The Heights	47 B1
The Manor	21 C4
The Maples	44 F1
The Marina	26 D1
The Marina	27 A2
The Marlings	37 C4
The Meadows	30 E1
The Mews	13 B4
The Mews	29 C1
The Orchard	22 F4
The Orchard (Bishopstown)	34 D1.4
The Orchards (Glasheen)	23 B4.2
The Orchards (Montenotte)	13 C4.9
The Orchards (Douglas)	38 E3
The Orchards (Mahon)	27 C3
The Ovals	39 B3
The Paddock	27 C3.4
The Paddocks	18 E4
The Paddocks	38 F3
The Square	19 A4
The Ridgeway	22 F4
The Rise	34 D3
The Village Green	26 E4.3
The Willows	38 D1
Thomas Ceannt Park	13 A3
Thomas Davis Street	12 F3
Thomas Street	24 D2.2
Thomond Square	25 A3.1
Thornbury Heights	40 D3
Thornbury View	40 D3

STREET NAME	PAGE / GRID REF
Thorndale	13 A1
*Thornhill Terrace (off Gardiner's Hill)	13 B4
Tiffany Downs	34 E3
Tivoli	26 F1
Tivoli Estate	26 E1
Tivoli Gardens	26 F1.1
Tobin Street	24 E2.7
Togher	35 C2
Togher Road	35 C2
Tonyville	25 A4.1
*Tonyville Mews (off Tonyville)	25 A4.1
*Tower Buildings (on Lower Glanmire Rd)	25 A1
Tower Street	24 E3
Townsend Place	24 E3
Trabeg Avenue	37 C2
Trabeg Lawn	37 C2
Trabeg Terrace	37 B1.6
Tracton Avenue	14 E4
Tracton Lawn	14 E4.1
Tracton Place	14 E4
Trafalgar Hill	26 E1
Tramore Lawn	37 C2
Tramore Road	35 C3
Tramore Road	36 E2
Tramore Villas	25 A4.10
*Tramway Terrace (East Douglas Street)	38 D2
Travers Street	24 E3.3
Tuckey Street	24 E2
Tudor Grove	31 A1
Tyrone Place	24 E3.1

U

STREET NAME	PAGE / GRID REF
Uam Var Avenue	33 C2
Uam Var Drive	33 C2
Uam Var Grove	33 C2
Union Quay	24 F2
University View	23 C3.16
Upper Kensington Road	39 C4
Upper Beaumount Drive	26 F3
Upper Cattle Street	24 D1.11
Upper Janemount Tce.	23 C1.3
Ursuline Cottages	27 B2.5

V

STREET NAME	PAGE / GRID REF
Valebrook	13 C2
Valentine Villas	24 D4.2
Vandeville	25 A4.6
Vandeville Terrace	12 E2.9
Verdon Place	25 A1.19
Verdon Row	25 B1.7
Vernamount View	37 A1.3
*Vernon View (on South Douglas Road)	37 A1
*Vesta Place (on Blackrock Road)	25 C3
Vicar Street	24 E3
Vicars Court	35 C2.2
Vicars Road	35 C2
Victoria Avenue	25 B3
Victoria Court	23 A3.7
Victoria Cross	23 A3.3
Victoria Road	25 A2
Victoria Street	13 A4.3
Victoria Terrace	23 A3.4
*Victoria Terrace (off Summerhill)	25 A1
*Victoria Terrace (on Alexandra Road)	13 A4
Victoria Village	23 A3.6
Victoria Villas	23 A3.1
Victoria Villas	23 A3.2
Victoria Villas	25 B3.9
View Villas	13 C4.11
*Vincent Place (Sunday's Well Road)	23 C2
Vincent's Avenue	12 E4.1
*Violet Ville (on College Road)	23 C3

W

STREET NAME	PAGE / GRID REF
*Waggett's Lane (off Ferry Lane)	24 E1.2
Wainsfort	39 A3
Waldin	37 C4
Wallace's Avenue	25 B4
Wallace's Row	27 C2
*Walsh Place (off Leitrim Street)	12 E4
*Walshes Square (off Devonshire St West)	24 D1.29

STREET NAME	PAGE / GRID REF	STREET NAME	PAGE / GRID REF	STREET NAME	PAGE / GRID REF
Wandesfort Quay	24 D2	Westbury Estate	35 A3	Windmill Road	24 F3
Wandesfort Street	24 E2.10	Westbury Grove	35 A3	Windsor Cottages	13 B4.10
Warburton Villas	24 D4.7	Western Road	23 A3	Windsor Place	13 B4.16
*Washington Court	24 D2.4	Western Road	23 C3	*Windsor Terrace	13 B4
(off Anne Street)		Western Terrace	23 C3.10	(on Ballyhooley New Rd)	
Washington Street	24 E2	Westgate Park	34 D2	*Windsor Villas	23 C3
Water Street	25 C1	Westgate Road	34 D1	(on Highfield Avenue)	
Watercourse Road	12 E4	Westlawn	35 A3.1	Winsley	23 B4.10
Waterfall Road	34 D3	*Westmere	23 C3	Winter Ville	24 D1.20
Waterfall Road	41 A1	(off Western Road)		Winter's Hill	24 D1.8
Waterloo Place	25 A1.2	Westside Estate	35 B3	Winthorp Lane	24 F2.10
Waterloo Terrace	25 A1.21	Westview	25 A4	Winthorp Street	24 F2.9
Waugh's Terrace	23 B2.5	Westview Terrace	24 D4.20	*Wise's Quay	24 D1
Well Road	38 D2	West Village	18 E4	(off North Mall)	
Wellesley Terrace	25 A1.8	Wherland's Lane	12 E3.4	Woburn Avenue	34 D1.1
Wellesley Terrace	25 A4.4	White Street	24 F3	Woburn Drive	34 D2
Wellington Avenue	23 C3.3	Whitebeam Road	35 C1	Woburn Place	25 B1.11
*Wellington Place	23 A2	Whiteoaks	35 A3	*Woburn Terrace	25 B1
(off Sunday's Well Rd)		Whitethorn	37 B1.1	(on Lower Glanmire Rd)	
Wellington Road	24 F1	Whitethorn Avenue	20 D4	Wolfe Tone Street	12 D4
Wellington Square	23 B4.1	Whitethorn Drive	20 D4	Wood's Place	24 F1.11
Wellington Terrace	23 A2.2	Whitethorn Grove	20 D4	Woodbine Lawn	20 D4
Wellington Terrace	25 B1.5	Widdering's Lane	24 E1.3	Woodbrook Avenue	34 E2
Wellington Villas	13 A4.19	William Street	24 F2.5	Woodbrook Drive	34 E2
Wellview	23 B3.9	*Willis's Place	13 A4	Woodbrook Grove	34 E3
Wenthworth Gardens	34 F2.4	(Youghal Old Road)		Woodbrook Road	34 E2
Westcliffe	18 E4	Willmount	13 B4.25	Woodford	21 C4.1
*West Cliffe	23 C3	*Willow Brook	46 D1.4	Woodgrove	37 B1.2
(on College Road)		(off Willow Close)		Woodhall	24 D4.19
Westcourt	18 D4	Willow Court	37 B1	Woodhaven	34 E3
West Douglas Street	38 D3	Willow Dale	27 B1	Woodhill Park	26 E1
Westgrove	18 D4	Willow Drive	18 F4	Woodhill Villas	26 E1.2
*West View	13 A4	Willow Lawn	25 C4	*Woodland View	13 B4
(on Military Hill)		Willow Lawn	37 C3	(Youghal Old Road)	
*West View	25 A4	Willow Park	37 C3	Woodland View	23 B3.10
(on Boreenmanna Road)		Willowbank	26 F3	Woodland View	25 A4.5
*West View	27 A3	Willowmere	39 C3	Woodland Villas	13 A4.4
(on Church Road)		Wilton Avenue	34 F1	Woodlands	45 A1
Westbourne Park	23 C3.2	Wilton Court	35 A2	Woodlands Drive	8 D4
Westbourne Terrace	24 D4.5	Wilton Gardens	23 A4	Woodlawn	22 F4
*Westbourne Villas	23 C3	Wilton Lawn	35 A1	Woodlawn	37 A1
(on Western Road)		Wilton Manor	35 A1.3	Woodlawn	35 C3.1
Westbrook Gardens	38 D3	Wilton Park Villas	34 F2.5	Woodlawn Mews	35 C2.6
Westbury Court	35 A3.4	Wilton Road	35 A1	Woodleigh Park	22 E4
Westbury Crescent	35 B3	Wilton Villas	35 A1.1	Woods Alley	24 D2.15
		Windermere Court	34 E2.3	Woods Street	24 D2

STREET NAME	PAGE / GRID REF	STREET NAME	PAGE / GRID REF	STREET NAME	PAGE / GRID REF
Woodvale Road	26 F4	Wycherley Court	24 D3·2	*Wyse's Cottages	24 D1
Woodview	35 D4	Wycherley Mews	23 C3·1	(off Blarney Street)	
Woodview	38 D1	Wycherley Place	23 C3·6		
Woodview	38 D2	Wycherley Terrace	23 C3·4		
Woodview	45 C1	Wyndham Downs	17 C4	York Hill	25 A1·5
Woodview	46 E2	Wyndwood	21 C4·2	York Street	24 F1
Woodview Terrace	13 B1·1	*Wynfield Mews	24 D1	York Terrace	25 A1·1
*Woolacomb Place	25 A2	(off Blarney Street)		Yorkboro	25 B3
(on Victoria Road)		*Wynneville	24 F4	Youghal Old Road	13 B3
Woolhara Park	37 B1	(on Evergreen Road)		Youghal Old Road	15 A1
Wrixon's Lane	12 E4·13				

Y

LIST OF STREETS NOT NAMED ON MAP BUT SHOWN BY SMALL NUMBER

PAGE / GRID REF	STREET NAME	PAGE / GRID REF	STREET NAME	PAGE / GRID REF	STREET NAME
10 F4	1 Coolmaine Cres.		5 Killeen's Green		9 Corkeran's Quay
	2 Hostel Complex		6 Kilnap Green		10 Berwick Lane
11 A4	1 Courtown Park	12 D3	1 Knockpogue Park		11 Broad Lane
	2 Courtown Drive		2 Farranferris Park		12 Madden's Buildings
	3 Kilkieran Close	12 D4	1 St Mary's Place		13 Seminary Buildings
	4 Foyle Avenue		2 School Avenue		14 Ardfert
11 B3	1 Dunnycove Cres.		3 School Place		15 Sunday School Lane
11 B4	1 College View		4 Plas Ceallachain		16 Farranferris Court
	2 Orrery Terrace		5 Plas De Barra		17 Rock Cottages
	3 Presentation Close		6 Kearney's Avenue		18 Mahony's Square
11 C1	1 Park Wood Close		7 Presentation Ave.		19 Millview Cottages
11 C2	1 Fairfield Square		8 St Philomena's Rd.		20 *Heyland's Lane
	2 Fairview		9 St Declan's Road		20 Blackpool Bridge
	3 Fairhill Heights	12 E2	1 St Michael's Road	12 E4	1 Vincent's Avenue
11 C3	1 Churchfield Gdns.		2 St Colman's Road		2 Convent Place
11 C4	1 Churchfield Place W.		3 St Brendan's Road		3 *Straw Hall
	2 Churchfield Tce. W.		4 Seminary Place		3 Farren Street
12 D1	1 Glenwood Drive		5 Bramble Cottages		4 Burke's Avenue
	2 Birchwood Close		6 Russell Court		5 O'Connell Street
	3 Elmwood Grove		7 Glenview Villas		6 St John's Square
	4 Beechwood Grove		8 Springview Terrace		7 Bleasby's Street
	5 Laburnum Grove		9 Vandeville Terrace		8 Allinett's Lane
	6 Ashwood Close	12 E3	1 Foley's Row		9 Hill Grove Lane
	7 Dierville		2 Arthur Villas		10 *Shandon Terrace
	8 Hazelville		3 Brocklesby Street		10 *Lr. Barrack View
	9 Bride Villas		4 Wherland's Lane		10 Church Avenue
12 D2	1 Fairfield Crescent		5 Dunloe		11 Emmet Place
	2 Farranferris Cres.		6 Seminary Villas		12 Cnoc Mhuire
	3 Close's Green		7 Aherlow		13 Wrixon's Lane
	4 Close's Park		8 Hattons Alley Lane		14 St Ann's Terrace

PAGE / GRID REF		STREET NAME
12 E4	15	St Mary's Avenue
	16	Cathedral Street
	16	*Chapel Hill
	17	Hodders Lane
	18	Rockwell Terrace
12 F1	1	Glenthorn Avenue
	2	Hawthorn Estate
	3	Marian Close
	4	Millfield Terrace
	5	Millfield Cottages
12 F2	1	St Francis Cottages
	2	Laffan's Court
12 F3	1	Mount Farran Place
	2	Prosperous Place
	3	Farran Cleary Place
12 F4	1	Sutton's Buildings
	2	Roche's Buildings
	3	Rathmore Buildings
	4	Goldsmith's Avenue
	5	Lady's Well Hill
	6	Sandymount Court
	7	Lansdowne Court
	8	Shandon View Cott's.
	9	Shandon Court
	10	St Mary's Villas
	11	Lansdowne Terrace
13 A1	1	Glenthorn Way
	2	Glenthorn Park
	3	Glenthorn Mews
	4	Glenheights Park
13 A2	1	Ballincollie Park
13 A3	1	Glenmount
13 A4	1	Mount Vernon Tce.
	2	Alexandra Villas
	3	Victoria Street
	4	Woodland Villas
	5	Charleville Cottages
	6	Centenary Row
	7	Cahill Ville
	8	Marian Ville
	9	Bellevue Terrace
	10	Roseneath Villas
	11	Mount Vernon View
	12	Egerton Villas
	13	Kimberley Villas
	14	Corban's Square
	15	Bellvue Terrace
	16	Sunmount
	17	Farnmore
	18	Shrewsbury Villas
	19	Wellington Villas
	20	Alexandra Place
13 B1	1	Woodview Terrace
13 B2	1	Meadow Park Close
	2	Meadow Park Grove
13 B3	1	Kelleher's Buildings
	2	St Mary's Avenue
	3	Sunview Place East
	4	Cahergal Villas
	5	Glenview Terrace
	6	Springmount Place
	7	St Anthony's Villas
	8	Grand View Place
	9	Cahergal Terrace
13 B4	1	Farleigh Place
	2	Smithgrove Terrace
	3	Richmond Avenue
	4	The Crescent
	5	City View
	6	Harrington Place
	7	Harrington Row
	8	Blarney View
	9	Harrington Square
	10	Windsor Cottages
	11	Gardiner's Hill Ave.
	12	Mary Ville Cottages
	13	*Ardpatrick
	13	Frankfield View
	14	Balmoral Terrace
	15	Mount View Tce.
	16	Windsor Place
	17	Hill View Villas
	18	Árd Aluinn
	19	Árd na Greine
	20	St Joseph's Terrace
	21	Belmont Terrace
	22	St Mary's Terrace
	23	St Mary's Place
	24	Rockspring Terrace
	25	Willmount
	26	Magdala Terrace
	27	Alma Villas
	28	Herbert Park Lawn
	29	Rockspring
	30	Carolina Terrace
	31	St Joseph's Villas
	32	Glenthorn Villas
	33	Alta Place
	34	Stream Hill
	35	Glenview Place
	36	Burton Place
	37	Ashton Place
	38	St Johns Terrace
13 C1	1	Meadow Park Drive
13 C2	1	Ashgrove Lawn
	2	Ashgrove Avenue
	3	Ashgrove Villas
	4	Ashgrove View
13 C3	1	Montenotte Grove
	2	Murmont Drive
	3	St Joseph's New Rd.
	4	Maymount Villas
	5	Glen View
	6	Murmont Villas
	7	Elm Grove Park
13 C4	1	Rockview Terrace
	2	Ashburton Hill
	3	Ascal San Criostoir
	4	Bealach San Criostoir
	5	Brian Dillon Crescent
	6	Clifton Road
	7	Clifton Avenue
	8	Leycester's Lane
	9	The Orchards
	10	Corkscrew Hill
	11	View Villas
14 D3	1	Murmont Close
	2	Murmont Grove
	3	Murmont Court
	4	Knights Court
	5	Mayfield Park
14 E2	1	Shamrock Grove
14 E3	1	Kerry Lawn
	2	Byefield Court
	3	Silver Spring Road
14 E4	1	Tracton Lawn
14 F3	1	Courtlands
15 A3	1	Lotabeg Green
21 C4	1	Woodford

PAGE / GRID REF		STREET NAME
21 C4	2	Wyndwood
22 F4	1	Convent Lane
	2	Bishopstown Park
	3	The Belfry
	4	Mount Carmel
	5	Kinloch Court
23 A1	1	Shanakiel Court
	2	Shanakiel Place
	3	Convent View
23 A2	1	Rose Hill
	2	Wellington Terrace
	3	Shannakiel Park
	4	Mount Prospect
	5	Lee View
23 A3	1	Victoria Villas
	2	Victoria Villas
	3	Victoria Cross
	4	Victoria Terrace
	5	Bridgeview Terrace
	6	Victoria Village
	7	Victoria Court
23 A4	1	Linaro Avenue
	2	Sheare's Avenue
23 B1	1	Ardmore Avenue
	2	Glandore Park
23 B2	1	Shanakiel Place
	2	Illen Villas
	3	Lower View Ville
	4	Soho Terrace
	5	Waugh's Terrace
	6	Shanakiel Lawn
23 B3	1	Marian Place
	2	Montford Park
	3	Salvador Place
	4	Carmelite Place
	5	Alacoque Place
	6	Bernadette Place
	7	Annaville
	8	Laurel Villas
	9	Wellview
	10	Woodland View
	11	Lucan Place
	12	Brighton Villas
	13	Bloomfield Terrace
	14	Castlewhite Apts.
	15	Sunnyside
	16	Redclyffe Terrace
	17	Carrigfern
	18	Fernhurst Villas
	19	Fernhurst Place
	20	Brookfield Villas
23 B4	1	Wellington Square
	2	The Orchards
	3	Robin Hill
	4	Coolowen Villas
	5	Fernhurst Terrace
	6	Brookfield Mews
	7	Aldergrove
	8	Ennismore Villas
	9	Fernhurst View
	10	Winsley
23 C1	1	Barrett's Buildings
	2	Model Cottages
	3	Upper Janemount Ter
	4	Mount Eden Rise
	5	Mount Eden Terrace
	6	Blair's Hill Square
	7	Lower Janemount Tce.
	8	Prospect Place
23 C2	1	Mentone Place
	2	College View Tce.
	3	Avondale
	4	Jamesville
	5	Carrigdhun
23 C3	1	Wycherley Mews
	2	Westbourne Park
	3	Wellington Avenue
	4	Wycherley Terrace
	5	Sunview Terrace
	6	Wycherley Place
	7	Mount St Joseph's View
	8	Eglinton Place
	9	St Mary's Place
	10	Western Terrace
	11	Dunedin
	12	Lucerne
	13	Laurel Hurst
	14	Mountpleasant
	15	Rock Villas
	16	University View
	17	College View
	18	Horgan's Buildings
23 C4	1	Croghtamore Square
	2	Lough View Terrace
	3	St Helen's Court
	4	Ashford Estate
	5	Sheraton Court
	6	Lapps Court
	7	Laurelmount
	8	Adare Villas
	9	Rosenheim
	10	Bellavista
	11	Loretto Ville
	12	Brendan Ville
	13	Homeville
	14	Innisfail
	15	Halcyon Villas
	16	Eileen Villas
	17	Auburn Villas
	18	Maybury
	19	Mount Prospect
	20	Landscape Terrace
	21	Monaville
24 D1	1	MacSwiney's Villas
	2	Father O'Flynn Pl.
	3	Brother Rice Ave.
	4	Ballymacthomas St.
	5	Allen Square
	6	St Theresa's Road
	7	Nicholas Lane
	8	Winter's Hill
	9	*Rock Cottages
	9	North Abbey Square
	10	North Abbey Street
	11	Upper Cattle Street
	12	*Hegarty's Square
	12	Nicholas Well Lane
	13	Buckley's Terrace
	14	Rock Well Lane
	15	Maymount
	16	Panorama Terrace.
	17	Panorama Tce. Upper
	18	River Lane
	19	Nicholas Hill
	20	Winter Ville
	21	Riverside Mews
	22	Glenryan Mews
	23	Friar's Avenue

PAGE / GRID REF		STREET NAME
24 D1	24	Parkmoor
	25	St Nicholas Square
	26	Ryan's Buildings
	27	Rock Villas
	28	Francis Street
	29	*Walshes Square
	29	Devonshire Street W.
24 D2	1	Moore Street
	2	Thomas Street
	3	Little Hanover Street
	4	*James Street
	4	Anne Street
	4	*Washington Court
	5	Mardyke Street
	6	Glochin Barra
	7	Prospect Row
	8	Coach Street
	9	Broad Street
	10	Inniscarrig Terrace
	11	Alverna
	12	St Vincent's View
	13	St Mary's Villas
	14	Palace View Place
	15	Woods Alley
24 D3	1	Gillabbey Park
	2	Wycherley Court
	3	Greenmount Place
	4	Greenmount Bldgs.
	5	Gillabbey Terrace
	6	Leary's Place
	7	College Square
	8	Honan Mews
	9	Crawford Mews
	10	Fullers Place
	11	Ardeevin
	12	Minerva Terrace
	13	Fairville
	14	Ard Na Naomh
	15	Altona
	16	Shamrock Place
	17	Maria Villas
24 D4	1	Lough Villas
	2	Valentine Villas
	3	Ardross Estate
	4	Ard na Rí Avenue
	5	Westbourne Terrace

PAGE / GRID REF		STREET NAME
	6	Ophelia Place
	7	Warburton Villas
	8	Ferndale Villas
	9	Centenary Crescent
	10	Greenmount Villas
	11	St Finbar's Terrace
	12	St Joseph's Terrace
	13	Skiddy's Homes
	14	Roselawn
	15	St Anthony's Villas
	16	Parnell Terrace
	17	St Mary's Villas
	18	St Francis Villas
	19	Woodhall
	20	Westview Terrace
24 E1	1	Knapp's Square
	2	Ferry Lane
	2	*Waggett's Lane
	3	Widdering's Lane
	4	Mahony's Place
	5	St Vincent's Place
	6	O'Connell Square
	7	John Philpott-Curran St.
	8	Eason's Avenue
	9	Chapel Street
	10	Cattle Market Ave.
	11	Curry's Rock
	12	Kyrl's Street
	13	Dalton's Avenue
	14	Half Moon Street
	15	Broguemakers Hill
	16	St Anne's Mews
	17	Cathedral Avenue
	18	St Rita's Villas
	19	Old Friary Place
	20	Brown's Hill
	21	Farren's Quay
	22	Exchange Street
	23	Gray's Lane
	24	Paul's Lane
	25	Little Market Street
	26	Corporation Bldgs.
	27	Francis Street
24 E2	1	Carey's Lane
	2	S.S. Peter & Paul's Pl.
	3	St Augustine Street

PAGE / GRID REF		STREET NAME
	4	Cockpit Lane
	5	St Peter's Avenue
	6	Grafton Street
	7	Tobin Street
	8	Christ Church Lane
	9	Kift's Lane
	10	Wandesfort Street
	11	Hanover Place
	12	Cross's Green
	13	Convent Place
	14	Meade Street
	15	Cross Street
	16	Portney's Lane
	17	French Church St.
	18	Mutton Lane
	19	Clark's Bridge
	20	Cross's Green Quay
	21	South Gate Bridge
	22	Nano Nagle Bridge
	23	Sober Lane
	24	Blackmore Lane
24 E3	1	Tyrone Place
	2	Keysers Hill
	3	Travers Street
	4	Prosperity Square
	5	Industry Place
	6	*St Stephen's Place
	6	Stephen Street
	7	James Square
	8	St Finbarr's Street
	9	St Nessan Street
	10	Annmount
	11	Maymount
	12	Crones Lane
	13	Step Lane
	14	Nicholas Church La.
	15	St Kevin's Square
	16	Evergreen Buildings
	17	Ardfallen Terrace
	18	Marguerita Villas
	19	*St Dominick's Tce.
	19	Frenche's Quay
	20	St Finbarr's Place
	21	South Rampart
	22	Red Bridge Mews
	23	St Dominick's Tce.

PAGE / GRID REF		STREET NAME

24 E4
1 Plas Mac Diarmada
2 Deerpark Court
3 Millbrook Lawn
4 Friars Walk Terrace
5 Maryville
6 St Anyhony's Villas

24 F1
1 Carrolls Quay
2 Harley's Street
3 Perry Street
4 Belgrave Avenue
4 *Sydenham
4 *Hansborough Place
5 Gordon Terrace
6 Elmwood
7 Hardwick Street
8 Bridge Street
9 St Patrick's Place
10 Sidney Place
11 Wood's Place
12 Little William Street
13 Belgrave Place

24 F2
1 Maryville
2 Deane Street
3 Faulkner's Lane
4 Drawbridge Street
5 William Street
6 Bowling Green St.
7 Merchant Street
8 Clontarf Street
9 Winthorp Street
10 Winthorp Lane
11 Caroline Street
12 Beasly Street
13 Phoenix Street
14 Crane Lane
15 Connell Street
16 Copley Place
17 Fitton Street East
18 Keeffe Street
19 Sraid An Athar Maitiu
20 Parliament Street
21 Anglesea Place
22 Pembroke Street
23 Terence McSweeny Qy.

24 F3
1 Stable Lane
2 Cotters Street

3 Margaret Street
4 *Morton Villas
4 Needham Place
5 Parkowen
6 East View Terrace
7 St John's Mews
8 Sawmill Lane
9 Drews Terrace
10 Nano Nagle Place
11 Maire Place
12 Langford Terrace
13 Frankfield Villas

24 F4
1 O'Connell Crescent
2 Murphy's Gardens
3 Erin Terrace
4 Deerpark Mews
5 Killingley Terrace
6 Kinsale Cottages
7 Ossory Place
8 Jessie Ville
9 Fernside Villas
10 Morningside
11 Ard Na Grena
12 Evergreen Villas
13 Maiville Terrace
14 St Joseph's Terrace

25 A1
1 York Terrace
2 Waterloo Place
3 Charlemont Terrace
4 Clifton Terrace
5 York Hill
6 Brian Boru Street
7 Beechmount Place
8 Wellesley Terrace
9 Grosvenor Place
10 Montpellier Place
11 King's Terrace
12 St Patrick's Presb'y.
13 Empress Villas
14 Empress Place
15 Summerhill Terrace
16 Adelaide Terrace
17 Mountain View
18 Summerhill Place
19 Verdon Place
20 Mount Verdon Tce.

21 Waterloo Terrace

25 A2
1 Anderson's Street
2 Hibernian Buildings
3 Geraldine Place
3 *Marina Villas
3 *Evenus Ville
4 *Electric Terrace
4 *Montenotte View
4 Eastville
5 Kingston Avenue
5 *Rosefield Terrace
6 Custom House St.
7 Monerea Terrace
8 Marina Terrace
9 Elizabeth Terrace
10 Park View
11 Old Station Road

25 A3
1 Thomond Square
2 Fitzgerald Place
3 *Anglesea Place
3 Anglesea Terrace
4 Flora View
5 *Knockrea Villas
5 Carrig View Terrace
6 Elm Park
7 Railway Cottages
8 Braemar
9 Knockrea Terrace
10 Holmwood Terrace
11 Eastcliff Terrace
12 Myrtle Ville
13 Elizabeth Place
14 Rockboro Court
15 Antonia Villas

25 A4
1 *Tonyville Mews
1 Tonyville
2 The Crescent
3 Railway Place
4 Wellesley Terrace
5 Woodland View
6 Vandeville
7 Roseville
8 South View
9 Laurelwood
10 Tramore Villas
11 Marble Hall Gardens

PAGE / GRID REF	STREET NAME
25 B1 1	St Luke's Avenue
2	Clarence Terrace
2	*Clarence Court
2	*Clarence Lodge
3	Barry's Lane
4	Grattan's Hill Lower
5	Wellington Terrace
6	Hackett's Terrace
7	Verdon Row
8	Sidney Terrace
9	Gibraltar Terrace
10	Magnolia Terrace
11	Woburn Place
12	Grattan's Hill
12	*Riverview Terrace
13	Nelson Terrace
14	Clahane Cottages
15	Lincoln's Place
25 B3 1	Haig Gardens
2	Clontymon Lawn
3	Sun Nook Park
4	Glenanaar
5	Arundel Villas
6	Arundel Terrace
7	Rockboro Terrace
8	Roseville
9	Victoria Villas
10	Sorrenta Villas
11	Grand View Terrace
12	Park Villas
13	Glenarm
14	St John's
15	St Joseph's Villas
16	St Joseph's Place
25 B4 1	Beechwood Drive
2	Knockrea Gardens
3	Chesterton Close
4	Knockrea Mews
5	Knockrea Drive
6	Cherry Drive
7	Elm Bank
8	Dryden Terrace
9	Dryden Place
10	Douglas Terrace
11	Annville
12	Ardeevin
13	Eldred Terrace
14	Belmont Place
15	Fernwood
16	Pinewood
17	Beachwood Place
18	Knockrea Lawn
19	Bryan Terrace
25 C1 1	Rockgrove Square
2	Rockgrove Terrace
3	Rockvale
4	Castleview Terrace Lr.
5	Castleview Terrace
25 C3 1	Ashton Place
2	Ashton Cottages
3	Allevard
4	Clonard
5	Ashton Ville
25 C4 1	Sunnyside
2	Elm Grove
3	Pic Du Jer Close
4	Dunedin
26 D1 1	Myrtle Hill Terrace
2	Bellvue Villas
26 D3 1	Goulden's Place
2	Ceanncora Lawn
3	Temple Lawn
4	Chiplee Villas
26 D4 1	Glencoo Park
2	Flaherty's Lane
3	Laurel Park
4	Our Lady of Lourdes Pk.
5	Somerton Drive
6	South Lodge Grove
7	Glencoo Gardens
8	Cogan's Cottages
9	Laurelville Cottages
10	Rock Lawn Terrace
26 E1 1	The Acres
2	Woodhill Villas
26 E2 1	Beaumont Lane
2	The Cottages
3	Maryville Mews
4	Mathew Place
5	Jamesville
6	Ardfoyle Place
7	Maryville Court
8	Clifton View
9	Beaumont Place
26 E3 1	St Gerard Majella Tce.
2	Marble Hill
3	Ardcairn View
4	Beaumont Cottages
5	Temple Hill Lawn
26 E4 1	Seamus Quirke Pk.
2	Carrigmore Park
3	The Village Green
26 F1 1	Tivoli Gardens
2	Castle Avenue
26 F2 1	The Cottages
2	Temple Gardens
3	Sunnyside
4	Rockcliffe Village
5	Carrigdubh Estate
6	Rockcliffe Terrace
26 F4 1	Silverdale Drive
2	Hettyfields Downs
3	Beaumount Court
4	Old Cliff
27 A2 1	Post Office Lane
2	Glandore Avenue
3	Rockgrove Estate
4	Dundanion Court
5	Ardnalee
6	Glandore Villas
7	Dundanion Terrace
27 A3 1	Barnstead Avenue
2	Avonlea Row
27 A4 1	Pine Court
2	Standard's Grove
3	Avonlea Gardens
27 B2 1	Factory Lane
2	Mahon Terrace
3	Convent Avenue
4	River View
5	Ursuline Cottages
27 B3 1	Convent Mews
27 C2 1	Ringmahon Close
2	Limes Avenue
3	Beechwood Close
4	Beechwood Court
27 C3 1	Ballinure Crescent
2	Ferney Close

PAGE / GRID REF		STREET NAME
27 C3	3	Loughmahon Close
	4	The Paddock
	5	Loughmahon Court
27 C4	1	Ballinure Lawn
28 D2	1	Lakeview Lawn
28 D3	1	Loughmahon Ave.
	2	Loughmahon Drive
	3	Ravensdale Close
	4	Island View
33 B3	1	Riverbank
33 C2	1	Oakgrove
33 C3	1	Pampas Grove
34 D1	1	Woburn Avenue
	2	Melbourn Mews
	3	Allendale Drive
	4	The Orchard
	5	Roslyn Court
34 D2	1	Foxford Avenue
34 D3	1	Dunville Villas
	2	Dunville Crescent
34 E1	1	Bishopscourt Hill
	2	Kenley Circle
34 E2	1	Firgrove Crescent
	2	Bishopscourt Ave.
	3	Windermere Court
	4	Laurel Court
	5	Pinewood
	6	Firview
	7	St Joseph's Gardens
34 E3	1	Stratton Pines
34 F2	1	Bishopscourt Park
	2	Bishopscourt Place
	3	Bishopscourt Way
	4	Wenthworth Gardens
	5	Wilton Park Villas
	6	Park Gate Villas
35 A1	1	Wilton Villas
	2	Glenarden
	3	Wilton Manor
35 A2	1	Summerstown Ave.
35 A3	1	Westlawn
	2	Brentwood Court
	3	Harley Court
	4	Westbury Court
35 B1	1	Clashduv Villas
	2	Glendale Avenue

PAGE / GRID REF		STREET NAME
	3	Glendale Road
	4	Tara Lawn
	5	Glendale Walk
	6	Birch Place
	7	Clashduv Place
	8	Clashduv Terrace
35 B2	1	Leamlara Close
	2	Ilen Court
	3	Blackwater Grove
	4	Maglin Grove
	5	Argideen Lawn
	6	Owenabue Close
35 C1	1	Hillside Avenue
	2	Hillside Grove
	3	Hillside Lawn
	4	Maple Place
	5	Ashford Estate
35 C2	1	Owenacurra Court
	2	Vicars Court
	3	Deanwood Place
	4	Shournagh Lawn
	5	Skiddy's Homes
	6	Woodlawn Mews
	7	Deanrock Terrace
	8	Don Bastible Court
35 C3	1	Woodlawn
36 D1	1	Carnog Mac Piarais
	2	Ardmanning Lawn
	3	Patrick O'Donoghue Pl.
	4	Father Dominic Place
	5	Pouladuff Place
36 D2	1	Michael Fitzgerald Rd.
	2	Marie Ville
	3	Sarahville Place
	4	The Acre
36 D3	1	Ardan an Riordanaigh
36 E2	1	Plas Ó Conghaile
	2	The Cottages
	3	Friars Court
36 F1	1	Hollyville
	2	Corran O Gramhna
37 A1	1	Hawthorne Villas
	2	Kilcolman Lawn
	3	Vernamount View
	4	Sunview Terrace
	5	Sunview Villas

PAGE / GRID REF		STREET NAME
	6	Palaceanne Villas
	7	Palaceanne Court
37 B1	1	Whitethorn
	2	Woodgrove
	3	Glen View
	4	Hillview Terrace
	5	Baltimore Lawn
	6	Trabeg Terrace
37 B2	1	Berkeley Court
37 C1	1	Elm Close
	2	Orchard Close
	3	Browningstown Park
37 C4	1	Kevington Close
38 D1	1	Hettyfield Mews
38 D2	1	Riverbank
	2	Clermont
38 D3	1	Grosvenor Mews
	2	St Patricks Terrace
	3	St Colomba's Tce.
	4	St Anthony's Villas
38 D4	1	Donnybrook Drive
	2	Shamrock Close
	3	Shamrock Drive
	4	Ballybrack Heights
	5	Grange Terrace
	6	Ardarrig Lawn
	7	Donnybrook Terrace
38 E1	1	Douglas Hall Mews
38 E3	1	Adare Mews
38 E4	1	Ardarrig Park
	2	Millbrook
45 B1	1	Hollyville Mews
45 C1	1	Grange Vale Court
46 D1	1	Calderwood Court
	2	James Connolly Place
	3	Ravenscourt Avenue
	4	*Willow Brook
	5	Cherry Grove
	6	Donnybrook Cottages
46 D2	1	Cherry Gardens
46 E2	1	Lyndon Crescent
	2	Melbourn Close

NOTES